THE MESSAGE
OF FAITH AND SYMBOL
IN EUROPEAN
MEDIEVAL BRONZE
CHURCH DOORS

THE MESSAGE
OF FAITH AND SYMBOL
IN EUROPEAN
MEDIEVAL BRONZE
CHURCH DOORS

Jadwiga Irena Daniec

Rutledge Books, Inc. Danbury, CT

Rutledge Books, Inc.
107 Mill Plain Road, Danbury, CT 06811
1-800-278-8533
www.rutledgebooks.com

Manufactured in the United States of America

Cataloging in Publication Data
Daniec, Jadwiga Irena
    The message of faith and symbol in European medieval
        bronze church doors

    ISBN: 1-887750-95-9

    1. Bronze Church Doors -- Medieval -- Religious symbols.

This Book is Dedicated
To the Memory
of My Husband, Juliusz Daniec

The author and the publisher wish to extend their thanks to *The Polish Review*, a quarterly published by The Polish Institute of Arts and Sciences of America, Inc., for granting its permission for the reproduction of some of the material included in this volume that had been previously published in *The Polish Review*: "The Bronze Door of the Gniezno Cathedral in Poland," vol. XI, 4 [1966], 10-65; "An Enigma: The Medieval Bronze Church Door of Płock in the Cathedral of Novgorod," vol. XXXVI, 1 [1991], 21-45; and "Man, Flora and Fauna in the Bronze Door of the Gniezno Cathedral in Poland," vol. XLII, 1 [1997], 3-27.

CONTENTS

LIST OF TABLES

CHAPTER ONE

The Message of Faith and Symbol in
European Medieval Bronze
Church Doors

As the first millennium drew to a close, much of
Christian Europe stood ready for the end of the
world. The year 1000 came and went, and the
architectural community, as if in relief, clothed the earth in
gratitude with a "white robe of churches," in the well-
known words of the eleventh-century monk Rodolphus
(Raoul) Glaber of the Order of Cluny.[1] Now, as we contem-
plate the close of a second millennium, it is perhaps fitting to
focus some attention on these monuments from ten centuries past, many of which survive to our times.

The extraordinary advances in large-scale sacral architecture in the eleventh and twelfth centuries in Europe
brought with them a return to and further development of a
monumental architectonic decorative system (unknown in
Western Europe since classical times), which can be seen in
the massive walls of the period.[2]

One important expression of this embellishment was the
ornamental bronze doors set in and framed by the decorative stone doorways of the church. But although they were a
popular manifestation of European taste in the eleventh and

twelfth centuries—roughly defined as the Romanesque period in medieval art[3]—very few ornamental bronze church doors representing that era exist today.

Twenty-four such doors, dating at least in part to the eleventh and twelfth centuries, can be found in twenty locations in Europe. Together they provide fascinating insights into medieval aesthetic and spiritual attitudes. The northernmost door is at Novgorod, near St. Petersburg in Russia; a second can be seen at Gniezno in Poland and in Germany the doors grace churches in Augsburg, Mainz, and Hildesheim. Most of the bronze church doors credited to the eleventh and twelfth centuries have been preserved in Italy, however: at Verona, Venezia, Pisa, Roma, Benevento, Montecassino, Troia, and Canosa; on the coast of the Tyrrhenian Sea, in the Gulf of Salerno, at Amalfi, Atrani, Ravello, and Salerno; on the coast of the Adriatic, in the region of the Gulf of Manfredonia, at Monte Sant'Angelo and Trani; and, finally, on the island of Sicily, at Monreale, near Palermo (Table I).[4]

In examining works of medieval Christian art, it is useful to reflect on their purpose and meaning to the people of that time; it was the intellectual and emotional response of the community to religious artistic expression that created the desire to have an ornamental bronze *porta* executed for a sacral building.

In the Middle Ages, the Christian Church took on a position of a new power in Western European civilization. Claiming ultimate authority over the entire Christendom, that eventually led to the split with the Christian East, the Church's spirit of proselytism engaged it in combating the teaching of doctrinal heresies, sanctioning holy wars, encouraging the rise of monasticism, and leading the faithful in an unfolding religious renewal. The Church became the "repository of Christian truth and spiritual experience," and had far-reaching influence over not only religious but political life.

A medieval church edifice was a symbol expressing the Christian culture of contemporary Europe—culture overarching all of society and a culture in which life at all levels was "imbued with the conceptions of faith." The second half of the eleventh century especially marked an increasing centralization of the Church, and intellectual activity intensified, based in monastic and ecclesiastic milieus. The progress of architecture and decorative arts depended on patronage, and that lay in the hands of institutions of political and economic power: the Church with its monasteries, Christian rulers, and the elite of the landed nobility and urban patriciate.[5]

Arranging for the erection of an ornamental door for a church edifice united, in that object of art, aesthetics, religious philosophy, and patronage in a comprehensive spiritual and communal act. The gift of a church door—a major article of faith—was both a tribute to the Divine and a reflection of the patron's piety; it also burnished the donor's reputation in the community.

A medieval church became a symbolic center for the communal system in its vicinity. It was a building of significance, large and lofty; it often sheltered relics of the saints, evoking intense spiritual fervor and devotion among the faithful and drawing to its site people on pilgrimage.[6] The portals of a church were not only a functional entry into the building (which sometimes afforded protection to fugitives seeking asylum in the sanctuary), but served as a backdrop for a variety of events in medieval Christian life—public meetings, debates, ceremonial processions, festivals of patron saints, markets, baptism and marriage celebrations, or even fulfillment of a publicly humbling penance.[7]

✠

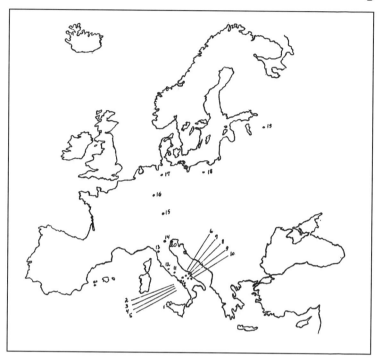

✠

TABLE 1

A GEOGRAPHICAL DISTRIBUTION OF THE
TWENTY-FOUR ELEVENTH AND TWELFTH
CENTURY ORNAMENTAL BRONZE CHURCH
DOORS IN TWENTY LOCATIONS IN EUROPE

1. MONREALE
2. AMALFI
3. ATRANI
4. RAVELLO
5. SALERNO
6. BENEVENTO
7. TROIA
8. MONTE SANT'
   ANGELO
9. CANOSA DI
   PUGLIA
10. TRANI
11. MONTECASSINO
12. ROMA
13. PISA
14. VERONA
15. AUGSBURG
16. MAINZ
17. HILDESHEIM
18. GNIEZNO
19. NOVGOROD
20. VENEZIA

Medieval Christian tradition, characterized by its ecclesiolatry, or worship of the church, invested the portal of the church edifice with special symbolism. The church doors, which faced members of the congregation as they entered the building, were seen as playing the role of a physical boundary between two different existential spheres: the sinful sphere of real life, outside the church, and the spiritual sphere of the church's interior. The crossing of the threshold represented passage between the two spheres. One left behind the outside world of the *profanum* and entered the church, a celestial realm, a holy enclave of the *sacrum*.[8] That passage articulated for the faithful their coming closer to the ultimate truth, which was God.[9] It is also believed that customs and observances of the time embellished church entrances with the "allegory of salvation,"[10] usually adopting Christological symbolism such as that found in the Good Shepherd parable and proclaimed in St. John's Gospel: "I am the door. If anyone enter by me he shall be safe...I am the door of the sheep..." (John 10:7-9). Thus, it may be seen how the mystery of religious faith demanded a splendid door for the entrance to the house of the Heavenly Sovereign, the *Domus Dei*, a door that may have been perceived as a "symbolic gate leading to heaven."[11]

In the visual culture of the Middle Ages, the church door's surface decoration was meant not only for the gratification of the sophisticated viewer's taste, but also to engage the imagination of the often unlettered onlookers— to teach, inspire, and prepare the faithful for their religious experience. The evangelizing Church of the era, serving as an arena for public communication and religious instruction,[12] utilized the door's decorative imagery as a vehicle for a message that could be recounted not only through words but also through a visual vocabulary of images, "significant mnemonic tools for the acquisition and transmission of knowledge."[13] Thus, the central function of the church door's imagery, simultaneously a creation in both plastic and literary arts,[14] was to serve not only as an object of decoration but also as the most effective means of articulating through its figurative language the teachings of the Church. Those Romanesque images may seem naïve, simple, and perhaps even humorous to the twentieth-century viewer at first glance, but they are solemn and hieratic, imbued with a suggestive force and the power to give a "concrete shape to every conception" and help the contemplative beholder to "apprehend spiritual reality through physical sight."[15]

The role of that special relationship between image beholders and images, arising "from concentrated gazing, from attentive prayer, and from sustained devotion,"[16] provided a "threefold reason" for the Church to create images that involved the faithful in dialectical processes. According to the thirteenth-century theologian and philosopher St. Thomas Aquinas, that threefold reason was: "First, for the instruction of the unlettered, who might learn from them as if from books; second, so that the mystery of the Incarnation and the examples of the saints might remain more firmly in our memory by being daily represented to our eyes; and third, to excite the emotions which are more effectively aroused by things seen than by things heard."[17]

This survey of extant eleventh- and twelfth-century bronze church doors, or their remnants, focuses on the door at the Cathedral of *Sancta Sophia* (*Sofīiskiĭ Sobor*) in Novgorod, Russia, and that at the Cathedral of Gniezno in Poland. The distinctive characteristics in their main decorative panel-fields distinguish these doors from others of their era.

In the Middle Ages, an artist and his work were viewed in a different light than they are today. Created by hands, artistic endeavors were regarded as manual labor and therefore considered inferior to occupations that required no physical effort for their accomplishment.[18] Consequently, medieval works were frequently executed by artist-craftsmen who were not identified as individuals—who engaged in their trade as members of communities, religious or lay, of anonymous artisans. Their religious creations were viewed as expressions of Christian *humilitas*, perhaps serving as a "penitential function" or an "acceptable form of meditation" contributing *ad maiorem Dei gloriam*.[19] As a sign of their devotion to the spirit of the work, the artists' creative output was generally unsigned; there was no clue pointing to the identity of its creators.

But medieval art was not always the "work of monks or of profoundly religious lay artisans inspired by a humble attitude of selfless craftsmanship and service to the Church." Notwithstanding their "humble social status as artisans,"[20] some medieval artists (contemporary medieval documents identify many of them, their travels, and interconnections) were fully aware of their talent, reputation and the respect they had earned for their craftsmanship, and did sign their work, affirming the "personal merit of their achievement."[21]

Only ten of the twenty-four eleventh- and twelfth-century bronze church doors discussed here were executed anonymously. The remaining doors bear inscriptions identifying the names of their creators, though some of the signs are no longer legible (Table II).

However, the door at the Cathedral of *Sancta Sophia* in Novgorod (1152-1154) is unique because its surface decoration recorded for posterity not only the names of its designers, but also the likenesses of those artists, rendered in bas-relief. It has been noted that the appearance of such portrait representations on a work of art was "impossible before the twelfth century and continued to be so for a long time following that century."[22]

The second example of a door noteworthy for its unique characteristics vis-à-vis Romanesque-era bronze church doors, or their remnants, on which this present survey has focused at length, is the door of the Cathedral of Gniezno (1170s or the last quarter of the twelfth century) in Poland, described by one eminent American art historian as an "important monument."[23] The iconographic program of the door's main pictorial panel-fields is unique in that they are devoted exclusively to just one theme: the biography of a saint, presented in a series of bronze bas-reliefs, arranged in the form of a continuous, unbroken narrative cycle, a narrative in which the selection and chronological arrangement of the images follow the progress of events as sequential biographical stages in the saint's life: "birth, upbringing, deeds and *acme*," in this case the saint's martyrdom.[24]

By contrast, none of the other doors of this era has a single iconographic program anchored in an unbroken narration based on one theme. Even those doors whose decoration was aimed at interpreting and glorifying saintly personages and holy episodes from the Old and New Testaments have their picture-fields arranged for the most part randomly. There is no strict chronological sequence in the selection and placement of individual images that is required for a continuous, pictorially presented narrative.

———— ✠ ————

TABLE II

UNSIGNED BY ARTIST-CRAFTSMEN: Atrani, the Church of San Salvatore del Bireto, 1087 (patron: Pantaleone, the son of Pantaleone Viarecta); Augsburg, the Cathedral of, circa 1050-60 or 1065; Benevento, the Cathedral of, 1150-1200; Hildesheim, the Cathedral of, 1015 (patron: Bernwardus, the Bishop of Hildesheim);

Montecassino, the Abbey of, 1066 (patron: Mauro, the father of Pantaleone, executed by Staurachios [?]); Monte Sant'Angelo, Santuario di San Michele, 1076 (patron: *Dominus* Pantaleone); Salerno, the Cathedral of, 1087-99 (patron: Landolfo Butrumile and his wife, Guisana Sebaston; Venice, the Basilica of San Marco: 1) the (main) Madonna Door, 1112-1138 (patron: Leo da Molino), and 2) the (right side) St. Clement's Door, circa 1100; Verona, the Basilica of San Zeno Maggiore, the late ninth to the late twelfth centuries (although unsigned, the artist of the older part of the door might have been Stefano Lagerinus; the names of Niccolò and Willelmus have also been suggested).

SIGNED BY ARTIST-CRAFTSMEN: Amalfi, the Cathedral of, before 1066 (1060-1065), executed by Simeone di Siria and Staurachios (patron: Pantaleone, the elder son of Mauro); Canosa, the Chapel-Mausoleum of Bohemund (Boemondo) I, 1111, probably executed by Rogerius Melfie (Amalfi [?]) Campanarum; Gniezno, the Cathedral of, 1170s or the last quarter of the twelfth century, probably executed by Luitinius and two others, not legible; Mainz, the Cathedral of, 988-1009, executed by Berengerus (patron: Willigisus, the Archbishop of Mainz); Monreale, the Cathedral of: 1) the main door, 1186, executed by Bonannus of Pisa, and 2) the side (northern) door, 1190, executed by Barisanus of Trani; Novgorod-Płock, the Cathedrals of, circa 1152-54, executed by Riquin, Waismut, and Avraam (possible patrons: Alexander of Malonne, the Bishop of Płock, or Vicmannus, the Bishop of Magdeburg); Pisa, the Cathedral of, circa 1180-86, executed by Bonannus of Pisa and Wilhelmus; Płock-Novgorod (see Novgorod-Płock); Ravello, the Cathedral of, 1179, executed by

Barisanus of Trani (patron: Sergio Muscetola); Rome, the Baptistery of St. John Lateran, 1195, executed by Pietro and Ubertino of Piacenza (Plaisance), (patron: Cardinal Cencio); Rome, the Basilica of St. Paul Outside-the-Walls, 1070, executed by Simeone and Staurachio Tuchitos of Scio and the designer Teodoro (patron: Malfigeno Pantaleone); Trani, the Cathedral of, 1175, executed by Barisanus of Trani; Troia, the Cathedral of: 1) the main door, 1119, executed by Oderisius of Benevento (?) (patron: Bishop Willelmus II), and 2) the side door, 1127, executed by Oderisius of Benevento (patron: Bishop Willelmus II).

The absence of any continuous narration tying a preceding picture-field to a subsequent one is especially noticeable in doors whose central panel images mix religious scenes with a variety of presentations of a nonreligious nature, such as heraldic emblems, figures clad in armor, or mythological figures; depictions of reptiles, birds, animals, and monsters, frequently entangled in symbolic confrontations with people; architectural, arboreal, and floral motifs; and rosettes and other geometric designs. On some of the doors, the principal, or component, panel ornamentation is in the form of inscriptions, repetitive series of the cross or cruciform symbols, Tree of Life motifs, or rows of single figures in ecclesiastical garb.

Such a diverse collection of designs renders each picture-field an isolated, finite decorative entity, rather than one of a series of images telling a story from its beginning to end. Consequently, anyone viewing most of the doors of this era sees each image singly, not as a component of a continuous narrative that would guide and sustain the viewer's attention in the reading of a pictorially presented story. That, indeed, is an experience unique to those beholding the decorative surface of the door of the Cathedral of Gniezno.

———— ✠ ————

NOTES: CHAPTER ONE

1 Henri Focillon, *The Art of the West* (London: Phaidon Press Ltd., 1963, two volumes), Vol. 1, *Romanesque Art*, p. 25.

Denise Jalabert, *La flore sculptée des monuments du Moyen Âge en France* [Sculptured Flora of Medieval Monuments in France] Paris: Éditions A. & J. Picard & Cie, 1965), p. 4.

Daniele Perla, *Le Porte di Bronzo di S. Michele sul Gargano, Santuariodi S. Michele* [The Bronze Doors of St. Michael on Gargano, Sanctuarium of St. Michael] (Monte S. Angelo: Edizioni PP. Benedettini, 1974), pp. 39-40.

2 Focillon, pp. 4, 105-111.

Tadeusz Dobrowolski, *"Rzeźba* [Sculpture], *966-1200," Historia sztuki polskiej* [History of Polish Art], edited by Tadeusz Dobrowolski, *Sztuka średniowieczna* [Medieval Art] (Kraków: Wydawnictwo Literackie, 1965, three volumes), Vol. 1, pp. 100-101.

3 Friedrich Heer, *The Medieval World, Europe 1100-1350* (Cleveland and New York: The World Publishing Company, 1961), pp. 315, 318.

George Savage, *A Concise History of Bronzes* (New York: Frederick A. Praeger, 1969), p. 87.

George Zarnecki, *Romanesque Art* (New York: Universe Books, 1971), pp. 5, 11.

Zarnecki, *English Romanesque Sculpture*, 1066-1140 (London: Alec Tiranti Ltd., 1951), p. 6.

4 However, it ought to be noted that some of the sources are excluding from that group the so-called Madonna Door and the door named after St. Clement at the Basilica of St. Mark in Venice, assigning them to the thirteenth or even sixteenth century (see Duard W. Laging, "The Methods Used in Making the Bronze Doors of Augsburg Cathedral," *The Art*

Bulletin [a quarterly published by the College Art Association] vol. 49 [1967], p. 130). It is also maintained that the door in the chapel of St. John Evangelist at the Baptistery adjacent to the Basilica of St. John Lateran in Rome represents the work of the early Christian period, perhaps of the fifth century, about 461-468 (see W. Eugene Kleinbauer, Review of *Le Porte Bronzée Bizantine in Italia* [The Byzantine Bronze Doors in Italy] by Guglielmo Matthiae, *The Art Bulletin*, vol. 56, no. 2 [1974], p. 280).

Bianca Maria Alfieri, *Il Duomo di Monreale* [The Cathedral of Monreale] (Novara: Istituto Geografico de Agostini, 1983), pp. 5, 7, 25-26; Plates 18, 22-27.

Kazimierz Askanas, *Sztuka płocka* [The Art of Płock} (Płock: Towarzystwo Naukowe Płockie, 1985, 2nd edition), pp. 50-61; Plates 540-546.

Askanas, *Brązowe drzwi płockie w Nowogrodzie Wielkim* [The Bronze Door of Płock in Great Novgorod] (Płock: Towarzystwo Naukowe Płockie, 1971), pp. 9-50; Plates 1-24.

Émile Bertaux, *L'Art dans l'Italie méridionale* [Art of the Southern Italy] (Paris: Albert Fontemoing, Éditeur; ouvrage publié sous les auspices de ministère de l'instruction publique, 1904, two volumes), Vol. 1, Part 1, pp. 316, 345-346, 364; Plate 1, Figure 153; Part 2, pp. 2, 51, 403-409, 414-416, 418, 421-429; Plate 18, Figure 176.

Albert von Boeckler, *Die Bronzetüren des Bonanus von Pisa und des Barisanus von Trani* [The Bronze Doors of Bonanus of Pisa and Barisanus of Trani] (Berlin: Deutscher Verein für Kunstwissenschaft, 1953, four volumes), edited by Richard Hamann, Vol. 4, Die Frühmittelalterlichen Bronzetüren [Early Medieval Bronze Doors] pp. 9-44, 47-70; Plates 1-131, 146-170.

Von Boeckler, *Die Bronzetür von San Zeno* [The Bronze Door of San Zeno] Vol. 3, Die Frühmittelalterlichen Bronzetüren, 1931, pp. 5-70; Plates 1-98.

Marie-Théodore de Bussierre, *Les Sept Basiliques de Rome* [The Seven Basilicas of Rome] Paris: Jacques Lecoffre et Cie, Éditeurs, 1846, two volumes), Vol. 1, pp. 137-319, 144-145.

O.M. Dalton, *Byzantine Art and Archaeology* (New York: Dover Publications, Inc., 1961), pp. 618-620.

Jadwiga Irena Daniec, "The Bronze Door of the Gniezno Cathedral in Poland," *The Polish Review*, vol. 11, no. 4 (1966), pp. 10-65.

Daniec, "An Enigma: The Medieval Bronze Church Door of Płock in the Cathedral of Novgorod," *The Polish Review*, vol. 36, no. 1, (1991), pp. 21-45.

Charles Diehl, *L'Art Byzantin dans l'Italie méridionale* [Byzantine Art in the Southern Italy] (Paris: Librairie de l'Art, 1894), pp. 237-238.

Tadeusz Dobrzeniecki, *"Joachim Lelewel jako historyk sztuki w świetle badań drzwi płockich i gnieźnieńskich"* [Joachim Lelewel as an art historan in light of research on the subject of the doors of Płock and Gniezno], *Biuletyn Historii Sztuki* [The Art History Bulletin] vol. 14, no. 1 (Warsaw, 1952), pp. 10-38.

Georges Rohault de Fleury, *Le Latran au Moyen Âge* [The Lateran in the Middle Ages] (Paris: Ve A. Morel et Cie, Éditeurs, 1877), pp. 150-151, 376-377.

Pierre Francastel, *"La porte de bronze de Gniezno"* [The Bronze Door of Gniezno], *L'Art Mosan* [Mosan Art] (Paris: Libraire Armand Colin, 1952), pp. 203-212.

Casimira Furmankiewicz, *"La porte de bronze de la cathédrale de Gniezno"* [The Bronze Door of the Cathedral of Gniezno], *Gazette des Beaux-Arts* [Fine Arts Journal] (Paris: vol. 3 {June 1921]), pp. 361-370.

Adolph Goldschmidt, *Die Bronzetüren von Novgorod und Gnesen* [The Bronze Doors of Novgorod and Gniezno] (Marburg am/Lahn: Verlag des Kunstgeschichtlichen Seminars der Universität Marburg A.L., 1932), Vol. 2, Die

Frühmittelalterlichen Bronzetüren, pp. 7-26, 39-41; Plates II/1-II/70; pp. 27-38, 41-42; Plates II/71-II/101.

Goldschmidt, *Die Deutschen Bronzetüren des Frühen Mittelalters* [The German Bronze Doors of the Early Middle Ages], Vol. 1, Die Frühmittelalterlichen Bronzetüren, 1926, pp. 12-38; Plates IX-CIII.

Kleinbauer, pp. 279-281.

Gustav Künstler, ed. *Romanesque Art in Europe* (Greenwich, Connecticut: New York Graphic Society, Ltd., 1968), pp. 134, 136, 172, 176; Plates 107, 128, 143-144.

Rev. Ryszard Knapiński, *"Drzwi płockie na tle innych brązowych romańskich drzwi kościelnych w Europie* [The Płock Door on the Background of Other Romanesque Bronze Church Doors in Europe], *Romańskie drzwi płockie, 1154—ok. 1430-1982* [A Romanesque Płock Door, 1154, circa 1430, 1982] (Płock: Towarzystwo Naukowe Płockie, 1983), pp. 12-29.

Laging, pp. 129-136; Plate 137.

Hermann Leisinger, *Romanesque Bronzes: Church Portals in Medieval Europe* (New York: Frederick A. Praeger, 1957), pp. 3-8; Plates 1-8, 10-160.

Joachim Lelewel, *"Drzwi kościelne płockie i gnieźnieńskie z lat 1133, 1155"* [The Church Doors of Płock and Gniezno from the Years 1133-1155], *Polska wieków średnich* [Poland in the Middle Ages], Vol. 4 (Poznań, 1851), pp. 261-329.

Adam Łapiński, *"'Wystawienie zwłok Św. Wojciecha' w drzwiach gnieźnieńskich. Próba określenia roli sceny w programie ikonograficznym zabytku,"* ["Displaying St. Wojciech's Remains" On the Gniezno Door. An Attempt to Define the Role of that Scene in the Iconographic Program of the Monument], *Biuletyn Historii Sztuki,* vol. 40, no. 2 (1978), pp. 95-103.

Alessandro Da Lisca, *La Basilica di S. Zenone in Verona* [The Basilica of St. Zeno in Verona] (Verona: Scuola Tipografica "Don Bosco," 1941), pp. 203-222; Figures 102-109.

Guglielmo Matthiae, *Le Porte Bronzée Bizantine in Italia* [The Byzantine Bronze Doors in Italy] (Rome: Officina Edizioni, 1971), pp. 14-15, 19-20, 29-30, 48-51, 55, 63-65, 67-89, 91-95, 97-107, 109; Plates 1-139.

Marian Morelowski, *"Les rapports artistiques et culturels de la Pologne avec les pays situés entre la Meuse et la Seine, du XIe au XIVe siècle"* [Poland's artistic and cultural relations with the territories situated between the Meuse and the Seine from the eleventh to the fourteenth century], *Cahiers Pologne-Allemagne* (Paris: Éditions Sarmatia, no. 2 [5], [Avril, Mai, Juin, 1960]), pp. 7-26.

Almerico Meomartini, *Benevento* (Bergamo: Istituto Italiano d'Arti Grafiche, 1909), p. 86; Illustrations 46-47.

Perla, pp. 31-33, 35-38, 43-53, 57-175 (including illustrations).

Thomas Jex Preston Jr., *The Bronze Doors of the Abbey of Monte Cassino and of Saint Paul's, Rome* (Princeton: University Press, 1915 [a dissertation presented to the Faculty of Princeton University in candidacy for the degree of Doctor of Philosophy]), pp. 8, 11-15, 17, 24, 26, 28-29, 31, 33-34, 41, 43, 45, 65-68; Plates I and II.

Joannis Ciampini Romani, *Vetera Monimenta* [Ancient Monuments] (Rome: Ex Typographia Joannis Jacobi Komarek Bohemi, apud S. Angelus Custodem, MDCXC, 2 volumes), Vol. 1, pp. 239-240, 280; Plate LXXIII.

Romańskie drzwi płockie, 1154 — ok. 1430-1982, pp. 7-151.

Savage, pp. 82, 85-86; Plates 59-61.

Jacques Stiennon, *"La Pologne et le pays mosan au moyen-âge: À propos d'un ouvrage sur la porte de Gniezno"* [Poland and the Mosan region in the Middle Ages: regarding the artwork on the Gniezno Door], *Cahiers de civilisation médiévale Xe-XIIe siècles* [Notebooks of the Medieval Civilization of the Tenth to the Twelfth Centuries] (Université de Poitiers: 1961), vol. 4, pp. 457-473.

Hanns Swarzenski, *Monuments of Romanesque Art* (Chicago: The University of Chicago Press, 1967, second edition), pp. 59, 78; Figures 264-268, 466-467.

Zygmunt Świechowski, *Romanesque Art in Poland* (Warsaw: Arkady, 1983), pp. 69-73, 265; Plates 189-209.

Michał Walicki, *"Dekoracja architektury i jej wystrój artystyczny"* [Architectonic Decoration and Its Artistic Endowment], in *Sztuka polska przedromańska i romańska do schyłku XIII wieku* [Polish Pre-Romanesque and Romanesque Art Until the Close of the Thirteenth Century], edited by Michał Walicki (Warsaw: Państwowe Wydawnictwo Naukowe, 1963-1968, two volumes), Vol. 1, part 4, pp. 227-230; Plates XI, 1144-1164, 1167-1195; Vol. 2, pp. 690-691, 743-744.

Drzwi gnieźnieńskie (The Gniezno Door), edited by Michał Walicki (Wrocław: Ossolineum, 1956-1959, three volumes).

Jan Zachwatowicz and others, *Katedra gnieźnieńska* [The Gniezno Cathedral], edited by Aleksandra Świechowska (Poznań: Księgarnia Św. Wojciecha, 1970, two volumes), Vol. 1, 187-192; Vol. 2, Plates 120-134.

Zarnecki, *Romanesque Art*, 39, 107-108, 120, 125; Plates 135-136, 138-140.

Zarnecki, *Art of the Medieval World* (New York: Harry N. Abrams, 1975), pp. 172, 175-176, 256, 261, 278; Plate 174.

Stanisław Mossakowski, *"La Porte de bronze de Gniezno et la 'Chronique polonaise' de maître Vincent"* [The Gniezno Door and the "Polish Chronicle" by Master Vincent] (Wrocław: Ossolineum, 1980), Vol. 2, pp. 11-29.

Mossakowski, *"Drzwi gnieźnieńskie a kronika polska Mistrza Wincentego"* [The Gniezno Door and the Polish Chronicle by Master Vincent] in *Sztuka jako świadectwo czasu* [Art as Testimony of Its Time] (Warsaw: Arkady, 1980), pp. 8-41.

5 Kenneth Clark, *Civilisation* (New York and Evanston:

Harper & Row, 1970), p. 35.

Focillon, p. 63.

Heer, pp. 318, 325-326.

Johan Huizinga, *The Waning of the Middle Ages* (New York: Doubleday & Company, Inc., 1954), pp. 151ff.

C.M. Kauffmann, *Romanesque Manuscripts 1066-1190* (Boston, Massachusetts: New York Graphic Society, 1975), p. 11.

6 Focillon, pp. 68-69.

Huizinga, pp. 151-156.

7 Lech Kalinowski, *"Treści ideowe i estetyczne drzwi gnieźnieńskich"* [Ideological and Aesthetical Themes in the Gniezno Door], in *Drzwi gnieźnieńskie*, Vol. 2, pp. 143-146.

Knapiński, pp. 12-15.

Łapiński, p. 103.

Walicki, *"Dekoracja architektury...,"* p. 227.

8 Aleksander Gieysztor, *"Przed portalem płockiej katedry"* [Before the Portal of the Cathedral of Płock], in *Romańskie drzwi płockie...*, p. 7.

Knapiński, p. 13.

9 Heer, p. 316.

Knapiński, pp. 12-15.

Marcia Kupfer, "Spiritual Passage and Pictorial Strategy in the Romanesque Frescoes at Vicq," *The Art Bulletin*, vol. 48, no. 1 (March 1986), p. 38.

Jacek Wierzbicki, *Drzwi gnieźnieńskie* [The Gniezno Door] (Warsaw: Arkady, 1979), p. 3.

10 Teresa Mroczko, *Czerwińsk romański* [The Romanesque Czerwińsk] (Warsaw: Auriga, 1972), pp. 30, 32, 38.

11 Dobrowolski, p. 118.

12 Marilyn Aronberg Lavin, *The Place of Narrative: Mural Decoration in Italian Churches: 431-1600* (Chicago and London: The University of Chicago Press, 1990), p. 15.

13 Brigitte Buettner, "Profane Illuminations, Secular

Illusions: Manuscripts in Late Medieval Courtly Society," *The Art Bulletin*, vol. 74, no. 1 (March 1992), pp. 78, 90.

14 Mossakowski, *"Drzwi gnieźnieńskie a kronika polska...,"* pp. 9, 32.

Knapiński, p. 15.

15 Herbert Kessler, "On the State of Medieval Art History," *The Art Bulletin*, vol. 70, no. 2 (June 1988), p. 186; see also Huizinga, pp. 152 and 200.

16 David Freedberg, *The Power of Images* (Chicago and London: The University of Chicago Press), pp. 320 and 470. Also, pp. 100, 159, 161-162 cite St. Thomas Aquinas's position (according to Freedberg's own translation from the Latin from *Commentarium Super Libros Sententiarum: Commentum in Librum III*).

17 Freedberg, p. 162; see also Buettner, pp. 79, 89.

18 Józef Lepiarczyk, *"Wstęp"* [Preamble] to *"Sztuka przedromańska i romańska, 966-1240"* [The Pre-Romanesque and Romanesque Art, 966-1240], in *Historia sztuki polskiej*, Vol. 1, pp. 46-47.

Zarnecki, *English Romanesque Sculpture*, p. 9. He maintains that documents throwing light on artists of the era, on their training, their organization, methods of work, or about the relationship between artists and their patrons are lacking. See also Rab Hatfield, review of "The Rise of the Artist in the Middle Ages and Early Renaissance," by Andrew Martindale, *The Art Bulletin*, vol. 57, no. 4 (1975), pp. 578-579. Compare the aforesaid views with the views of Kessler, pp. 181-182.

19 Kalinowski, *"O nowo odkrytych inskrypcjach na drzwiach gnieźnieńskich"* [About the Newly Discovered Inscriptions on the Gniezno Door], *Drzwi gnieźnieńskie*, Vol. 2, p. 393.

Kessler, pp. 179-180.

20 Meyer Schapiro, "On the Aesthetic Attitude in Romanesque Art" (*Art and Thought*, London [August 1947]),

Romanesque Art, Selected Papers by Meyer Schapiro (New York: George Braziller, Inc., 1977, three volumes), Vol. 1, pp. 3, 22.

François Masai, *"Les manuscrits à peintures de Sambre et Meuse aux XIe et XIIe siècles"* [Illuminated Manuscripts from the regions of Sambre and Meuse in the eleventh and the twelfth centuries], *Cahiers de civilisation médiévale Xe-XIIe siècles*, 1960, vol. 3, pp. 181-182, 187.

21 Schapiro, "On the Aesthetic Attitude...," pp. 22-23.

Schapiro, "On the Relation of Patron and Artist: Comments on a Proposed Model for the Scientist," (1964) in *Theory and Philosophy of Art: Style, Artist, and Society, Selected Papers by Meyer Schapiro* (New York: George Braziller, Inc., 1994, four volumes), Vol. 4, pp. 228-229.

Kalinowski, *"O nowo odkrytych inscrypcjach...,"* pp. 393, 398-399, 402, 406-408.

Kauffmann, p. 15.

Knapiński, pp. 17, 21-25, 27.

Morelowski, *"Drzwi gnieźnieńskie, ich związki ze sztuką obcą a problem rodzimości"* [The Gniezno Door, Its Links with Foreign Art and the Problem of Nativism], *Drzwi gnieźnieńskie*, Vol. 1, p. 44.

Askanas, *Brązowe drzwi płockie...*, p. 11.

Zofia Budkowa and Adam Wolff, *"Napis na listwie drzwi gnieźnieńskich. Analiza wstępna. Uwagi paleografa"* [The Inscription on the Molding of the Gniezno Door. An Introductory Analysis. Paleographer's Remarks], *Drzwi gnieźnieńskie*, Vol. 2, pp. 387-390.

Dalton, pp. 619-620.

de Fleury, p. 151.

Gieysztor, *"O napisach na drzwiach gnieźnieńskich"* [About the Inscriptions on the Gniezno Door], *Drzwi gnieźnieńskie*, Vol. 2, pp. 415-418.

Perla, pp. 35-36.

Walicki, p. 229.

Zarnecki, *Romanesque Art*, pp. 107-108, 125.

22 Gieysztor, *"Przed portalem płockiej katedry,"* p. 10. Kauffmann, p. 25. But, according to him, the continental illuminators, such as Norman artists Hugo Pictor and Robert Benjamin, had drawn portraits of themselves in ornamental initials already in the second half of the eleventh century.

23 Schapiro, "The Bowman and the Bird on the Ruthwell Cross and Other Works: The Interpretation of Secular Themes in Early Medieval Religious Art," *The Art Bulletin,* vol. 45, no. 4 (1963), p. 352.

24 Henry Maguire, "The Art of Comparing in Byzantium," *The Art Bulletin,* vol. 70, no. 1 (March 1988), pp. 88-89, 91, 93-94, 98, 102. He seeks the prototype of a presentation so structured of a visual narrative in medieval works of art (both sacred and secular) in the rules and techniques of a "rhetorical *encomium,"* as practiced by Byzantine painters in their art of pictorial narratives.

CHAPTER TWO

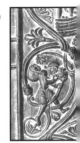

Man, Flora and Fauna in the Bronze Door of the Gniezno Cathedral in Poland

I n Central Poland, about thirty miles northeast of the city of Poznań, lies Gniezno, one of the oldest Polish urban communities and the legendary cradle of the Polish nation. Dating back to an eighth-century settlement, it was referred to as a *civitas* as early as the eleventh century.[1]

The Cathedral of Gniezno, a fourteenth-century Gothic edifice erected over the foundations of two earlier churches built between the tenth and twelfth centuries, possesses an ornamental door, made of bronze, that is much older than the cathedral (Figure 1).[2] It is regarded as a twelfth-century monument and an extant part of decoration of the earlier Romanesque basilica that was on the present cathedral's site.[3]

The door's decoration represents an iconographically unique program not observed in other bronze church doors of the era. The subject of the decoration is a continuous narrative recounting, in a series of relief carvings, the life and martyrdom of Saint Adalbert (Święty Wojciech), one of Poland's patron saints and a tenth-century missionary who, like his predecessors Saints Patrick, Boniface, Columba (or Augustine), and Martin of Tours, distinguished himself in the evangelization of the European continent.[4]

The Gniezno door's pictorial biographical narrative is contained within a cycle of eighteen rectangular panel-fields of bronze, nine on each surface of the door's two wings.[5] Filled with carvings in relief, the panels are placed one above the other, and separated from one another by narrow slightly convex strips of unadorned bronze.

The Gniezno door's narrative (Table III) inspires a constant feeling of passage from one event to the next, a feeling of emergence and development of the story, written in images instead of in words.[6]

On the left wing, the scenes unfolding upward from its bottom to its top in a continuous movement of ascent and "becoming," are imbued with an atmosphere of quiet and serenity. Beginning with the future saint's birth, the scenes show a gradual growing of the man, in both the physical and spiritual senses. Then, when the narrative process transfers to the right wing, the series of events is read from the top downward. These scenes are filled with a sense of increasing intensity, conflict and drama. There is a rhythm in the descent: The man's mission is undertaken and fulfilled, culminating in his death as a martyr; the final four panels show the disposition of his remains.

The first image of the narrative, a scene in which a newborn is given his first bath, records the birth of Wojciech in Libice, Bohemia. Continuing in an upward direction, the second scene depicts his being presented by his parents at the church in Libice. In the next scene, he is entering the cathedral school in Madgeburg (it has been said that during his Confirmation, Archbishop Adalbert of Magdeburg named the boy after himself, and it was under the name of Adalbert that Wojciech gained his fame in the Christian world). In the subsequent scene, Adalbert is depicted praying in solitude, filled with a desire to devote himself to the service of God. When Adalbert becomes Bishop of Prague in 983 (his investiture took place in Verona), he is shown receiving a bishopric from the hands of the German Emperor Otto II. The next scene shows him healing a devil-possessed man. The following panel depicts Adalbert having a dream in which the vision of Christ appears to him. Then he is seen pleading before a ruler on behalf of the people in bondage. Adalbert is next shown performing a miracle (involving a dropped but unshattered vessel) during his sojourn in the Benedictine monastery of St. Boniface and St. Alexis on the Aventine Hill in Rome. Adalbert stayed in that monastery and in the monastery of Montecassino for several years after he left Prague in protest against the behavior of his flock there. Later, he returned to Prague and eventually, after a visit in Hungary, went to the Baltic Sea territories, under the aegis of the Polish ruler Bolesław Chrobry (Boleslaus the Brave), to convert the local pagan population to Christianity. This mission is represented on the right wing of the Gniezno door.

At the top of the wing and continuing downward to the bottom, the narrative shows Adalbert's arrival among the pagan Prussians of Pomerania; he and his four companions approach the shore in a rowboat and encounter a group of armed hostile Prussians. The next two scenes present Adalbert at the start of his evangelical mission baptizing the Prussians and, later, preaching to them—while the Prussians' stance betrays their opposition to him. The following panel depicts Adalbert celebrating the Mass which was to be the last one said by him. In the succeeding scene, he is attacked and killed (this tragic event took place in 997). The next panel depicts the martyr's remains being displayed. Later, Bolesław Chrobry is shown paying ransom for Adalbert's body. Following this act, Adalbert's remains are brought to rest in the abbey in Trzemeszno, in the vicinity of Gniezno, and finally to Gniezno itself. The last scene represents deposition of Adalbert's remains at the Cathedral of

Gniezno. After his canonization in 999, the tomb of Adalbert became the site of the saint's cult and a place of pilgrimages.[7]

TABLE III

The Pictorial Narrative of the Life of St. Adalbert
It begins at the bottom of the left wing, unfolding in an upward direction to its top. It then transfers to the right wing, continuing downward from the top to the bottom of the wing.

9. The miraculous intercession of Adalbert in the monastery of St. Boniface and St. Alexis on the Aventine Hill in Rome.

8. Adalbert pleading before a ruler on behalf of the people in bondage.

7. Adalbert's dream in which the vision of Christ appears to him.

6. Adalbert healing the possessed.

5. Investiture in Verona of Adalbert as Bishop of Prague by the German Emperor Otto II.

4. Adalbert praying in solitude.

3. Adalbert entering the cathedral school at Magdeburg.

2. Adalbert being presented by his parents at the church in Libice.

1. Birth of Adalbert.

10. Adalbert's arrival among the pagan Prussians.

11. Baptism of the Prussians.

12. Adalbert preaching to the Prussians.

13. Adalbert celebrating his last Mass.

14. Martyrdom of Adalbert.

15. Displaying of the martyr's remains.

16. Ruler of Poland, Bolesław Chrobry, paying ransom for Adalbert's body.

17. Transportation of Adalbert's remains on the way to Gniezno.

18. Deposition of the remains at the Gniezno Cathedral.

Two door knockers made of bronze and sculptured in the form of lion heads holding rings in their mouths mark the middle register of the wings of the door of the Gniezno Cathedral.[8]

Each of the wings is framed by a wide, richly ornamented border, surrounding the door's central pictorial narrative of St. Adalbert's life. Rendered in bronze bas-relief, the border is filled with a *rinceau* (foliage) pattern, a spiraling vine-like stem adorned with motifs whose forms, devoid of religious content, are evocations of the world of nature, mingling naturalistic representations of flora, fauna (Figure 2), and human figures (Figure 3) with fantastic species of the animal and botanical worlds (Figures 4-6).[9]

The eighty-five convoluting scrolls of the *rinceau* are a setting for a vegetal world (Table IV) which at first glance appears to evoke the forms of nature but does not represent true botanical genera. Although they are based on nature, and imbued with an inner organic vitality characteristic of natural flora, most of the forms are invented, abstractions of motifs found in nature, influenced by imagination. One may say, using the expression of the French medieval art historian Denise Jalabert, that in the Gniezno *rinceau* 's plant life *"la flore est vivante avant d'être vraie"* [the flora is alive before being real], a characteristic of foliate forms popularly represented in artistic compositions between the years 1140 and 1170.[10]

It was once observed that the presence of plantlike ornament on works of art might be compared to the role that natural flora play in true life, by bringing into reality the elements of "beauty, joyfulness and charm." For what would life be, what would the earth be without the flowers and foliage? What would artistic works be without floral sculptural ornamentation?[11]

The plant world of the Gniezno *rinceau* is frequently depicted in entanglement with the animal world. This allows the transformation of anatomical extremities, such as tails or tongues, into vegetative elements and permits the vegetal elements to cut across the animal forms. "It is as if the barriers between the animal and vegetable kingdoms had been cast down, and plants could turn into animals, animals into plants, at random."[12]

The animals of the Gniezno *rinceau* belonging to the natural world (Table V) include lions and monkeys, a stag, a goat, a squirrel, a hare, a dog, a wolf, a rooster, a raven, long-legged waterbirds, and several small birds which, although unidentified as to species, are nonetheless portrayed as true forms of nature.

Zoomorphic forms of the fantastic kind (Table VI) are hybrids born of both imagination and the world of nature. Their improbable shapes, embodying characteristics of real-life birds, beasts and reptiles, sometimes incorporate the qualities of man. There are multiple representations of a winged biped, part dog, part bird, part reptile; of various mammals; the centaurs; there is a quadruped with the head of man; a human-headed winged reptile; a mammalian-winged biped; half-mammal and half-reptile hybrids; a mammal with the head of a bird; a bird-reptile creature; and serpents bearing canine heads.

This multiform botanical-zoomorphic background of the *rinceau* is inhabited by nine human-figure motifs (Table VII).

The Romanesque aesthetic principle in church art had called for the interweaving and fusing of religious images or text with decorative elements possessing no religious content, that is, the designs were both naturalistic and fantastic, in which themes combining the human, plant and animal worlds played a characteristic role. Such ornamental motifs were common and widespread at that time: They were executed in bronze or precious metals; ivory carvings; works of

✠

enamel and embroidery; stained glass; wall paintings; sculptured stone of church portals, lintels, jambs and capitals; and woodwork decorating the undersides of seats in church stalls. They also appeared as part of the initials and ornamental borders on the pages of illuminated manuscripts.

The gradual emergence of the elaborately decorated Romanesque initial in book illumination became a discernible trend in the latter part of the eleventh century (after occasional appearances in the tenth century) and eventually reached its peak during the first half of the twelfth century. Its dominant decorative motif consisted of spirals of foliage within which were enmeshed forms representing animals, beasts, birds and dragons. Later artistic invention incorporated human figures into this ornamentation, often in combat with the animal world.[13]

In the European continent's medieval culture, the skills of reading, writing and interpreting text were seen as awe-inspiring, meaningful faculties. The letter itself, regarded as the symbol of teaching and the source of knowledge, was conceived of as representing a living form. In the hands of the medieval artist, the letter virtually comes to life, transformed by its embellishments—fashioned out of the living forms of nature: human, animal, bird and plant—into a living form.

But the text of a medieval story, similar to a text of our own time, could be recounted not only by verbal means, but also through pictorial representation, an image substituting for a letter. Like an ornamental letter, an image became a symbol of teaching that was transformed into a living form by its decoration with human, animal, bird and plant forms. The Romanesque artists' dislike for bare, unadorned space (*horror vacui*), combined with their search for designs of decorative richness and diversity, led them to invent new motifs and combinations that were "literally inexhaustible."[14]

Many of the inquiries into decoration in medieval religious art are accompanied by an examination of one question: whether or not there is any thematic bond between the central religious theme imagery of an artistic work and the marginal decorative details of nonreligious themes which embellish that imagery. Was the selection of marginal decorative details an "accident, incident or intention?"[15] And, assuming that there was a meaningful bond between the two elements, how might the viewers of the work of art interpret this existence of a mutual reference? To what extent does the marginal decorative element participate in the telling of the central religious theme imagery of the work? To what extent does the ornament based on nature fulfill the role of "mediator" between works of art and their viewers or users?[16] To suggest a solution to these questions, a pictorial language of Romanesque decorative themes uniting plants, monsters, animals and human figures remains undeciphered, for "there is some uncertainty about how to look at it, how to see it, and, therefore, how to interpret it."[17]

To Romanesque-era contemporaries such as Theophilus, a twelfth-century monk-artist and the author of *De Diversis Artibus*, the branches, flowers and leaves, as well as little animals, birds, vermicular patterns and nude forms were an enrichment of sacred texts for the greater glory of God, even if such "enrichment" was devoid of a deeper meaning.[18]

Another person of the same era, St. Bernard (1090-1153), a great Cistercian abbot of Clairvaux, monastic ascetic and reformer, regarded excessive decoration in monastic churches as "unbridled, often irrational fantasy," opposed to monastic spirituality, satisfying only the spectators' "idle curiosity."[19]

A contemporary of St. Bernard, Suger (1081-1151), the abbot of St. Denis, Regent of France and patron of arts, ardently promoted art as the material means, in his view, to

✠

aid spirituality in the faithful. But it was precisely that function which St. Bernard felt was useless in arts of decoration, distracting the faithful from worship.[20]

To such twentieth-century art historians as Henri Focillon, that imagery so "abundant in monsters, visions, and enigmatic symbols" represents a "tumultuous mêlée," seemingly emanating from the "caprice or delirium of a solitary visionary," disconcerting the onlooker with both its composition and its sentiment. Similarly, Ernst Gombrich comments on "ridiculous monsters" as "elusive dream-imagery" and a "waste and frivolity."[21]

In Poland, two prominent art historians, Lech Kalinowski and Zdzisław Kepiński, proposed that the placement of ornamentation—that is, of the vegetal and animal forms used as the adornment of a religious image—was replete with symbolic significance. They argued that the creators of the border in the Gniezno door perceived an "allegoric sense" and a "moralizing symbolism" in their choice of certain figural human, animal and plant motifs with which they embellished the border, and also in the judicious manner in which they placed and juxtaposed these marginal ornamental motifs against the door's principal religious images.[22]

The Polish scholars said that even though not all of the border's ornamental motifs suggestively manifest the symbolism of a theologically moralistic context, the artists' aim was to use the border's imagery, surrounding the dramatic narration of the life of St. Adalbert, as an accompanying commentary in a metaphorical sense. One perceives the attempt to unify the ornamental world of the border with the central religious imagery of the door. That analogy and reciprocal tie between the two elements of the door's total surface decoration appear to have been based on a subtle understanding of a psychological situation hidden in historical episodes of the saint's life and in the symbolic essence of the selected ornamental elements of the framing border.[23]

Thus, according to Kalinowski and Kępiński, the door's overall decorative schema helped to express in the language of poetic parable the ideas of philosophical dualism existing in the domains of spirit and matter. It communicated to the onlookers the notion of moral dualism of evil versus the endangered good, and the basic conceptions of God and Satan, sanctity and sin, heaven and hell.[24]

Polish art historian Stanisław Mossakowski remarked that through a keen, joyous observation of a natural world of man, animal and plant, the medieval mind was shown a way to gain a deeper cognition of the Creator.[25] That process "served as a reminder of humanity's oneness with God and his creations," observed an American scholar, J.L. Schrader.[26] Both Schrader and the French medievalist Louis Réau suggested (on the basis of the views explored and shaped in the writings of some philosopher-theologians of the Middle Ages)[27] that medieval society—in its quest for both simple metaphors and elaborate allegorical interpretations "in terms of a pattern for life and salvation through Christ"[28] — had sought an explanation of truths essential to faith not only in sacred writings, but also in physical signs of the world of nature and in historical events experienced by humanity. The phenomena of the visible world had been perceived as fraught with some deeper, concealed sense, cloaking and simultaneously revealing symbolically a world that remained physically invisible.[29] It was the world of God's will, of the universal law of nature and of the process leading the human mind upward from material things to the immaterial to the transcendental reason of "harmony and light" which is God.[30]

The point of view that made the visible and invisible worlds inseparate and connected, that linked human nature with divine design, contributed to envisaging an association between elements in the world of nature and symbolism invested with theological interpretation.[31] Medieval beliefs about animals, regarded with curiosity, admiration, awe, and fear, especially excited the imagination, creating the "animal myth." Their "habits and peculiarities" became rich in sacred symbolism.[32] The animal worlds of real life and of the realm of human fantasy had been studied not for themselves alone, but as a reflection of man, the center of the Creation. The animal world had come to be regarded as a "mirror of human morals," reflecting the passions, virtues and vices of the human race.[33]

Consequently, a medieval artist tended to create animal-form designs not only purely for decorative purposes; he also pictured them as symbolic figures, and so he assigned human traits to animals and animal traits to people, investing these traits with moralizing conceptions and teachings often tinged with humorously inventive, penetrating insight. It has been observed that in medieval thinking no difference separated a naturalist from a moralist,[34] even though "knowledge" of the natural world, being compiled from ancient texts and contemporary (medieval) descriptions and factual observations, often mixed facts with myth and produced fictitious, imaginary notions.[35]

Polish scholars Aleksander Gieysztor and Mossakowski see the "allure of an intellectual adventure,"[36] a diversion stimulating the observer's eye, his mind as well as the heart, in the process of interpretation of symbolic meanings, of symbolized ideas.

A "symbol," as defined by Arnold Hauser, a sociologist of art, is a "form of indirect representation that does not call a thing by its name [and] avoids straightforward description in order either to disguise or to reveal it in a more striking way, or even, perhaps, to disguise and reveal it at the same time."[37] According to him, "there is, no doubt, in every kind of artistic symbolism an element of mystery and mystification," of ambiguity and variety of possible interpretations.[38]

The complex ways in which meanings were not always perfectly or not immediately clear, yet attempted to convey notions of "allegoric sense" and "moralizing symbolism," are illustrated by the following examples of a zoomorphic form ornamentation, in which anthropomorphism, or characteristics and emotions of humans, were projected onto animals. Nonreligious in theme, they became moralizing in intention, exploring a symbolic interaction between humans and animals.

The lion, a king of the animal world, was sometimes interpreted as both a symbol of Christ and a symbol of courage.[39] When the lion's head motif was used for the door pulls of medieval sacred buildings, the lion was often regarded as a guardian of the sanctuary and a symbol of power, authority, and the immunity of the church.[40] The lion's form may have also served as a symbolic admonition: "Be sober and watch, because your adversary, the devil, as a roaring lion, goeth about seeking whom he may devour" (I, Peter 5:8). Or, it could have been translated into a symbolic invocation: "Deliver me from the lion's mouth" (Psalm 22:22).

A rooster was the emblem of Christ triumphant, or vigilance, and the call to penance; a peacock represented pride and arrogance; a crane was thought to keep a watchful guard.[41] The dog's nature was believed to be sagacious, for by rejecting error the dog finds truth; the dog was also the symbol of fidelity, but it could also symbolize uncleanliness. A squirrel represented the symbol of covetousness; the centaur, one of the incarnations of the devil, it was said, also personified a warning against evil, having the simultaneous power of deterring from it; it was a lustful animal, seldom seen by men—its body was formed like that of a horse, but from the belly upward it was shaped like a man.[42] The wolf, to which the "devil bears the similitude," "snatches and scatters the sheep" (John 10: 11-13); it is the symbol of greed and of force and demonism.[43]

A fantastic creature with the head of a man and a lion's body hissed like a serpent and was described as hankering after human flesh "most ravenously."[44] It was closely related to the basilisk, another imaginary monster. This one, a hybrid—part avian, part reptilian and serpentine—was thought to have been able to destroy a man if it only looked or breathed at him.[45]

The motif of a stag, the embodiment of good, called to mind the expression from David's Psalm 42:2: "As the hart panteth after the fountains of waters, so my soul panteth after Thee, O God.[46] To the serpent, generally associated with the demonic aspects temptation and sin, was also attributed, in some contexts, the virtue of prudence.[47] A siren, or harpy, part bird, part serpent with a man's head, meant impurity; it was able to entice people and to put them to sleep; it also symbolized souls of the dead.[48] The asp, a serpent combined with a canine head, was a symbol of evil and sin; it dangerously injected poison with its bite: "Adders' poison is under their lips" (Psalm 140:4). The reptilian world was generally regarded as symbolic of the anti-thesis of good. A dragon, a winged creature, part dog and part reptile, was, along with the monkey, compared to the devil; a raven dealt with the "troubles of men through omens," it disclosed the paths of treachery and predicted the future; a goat "can see so very acutely" that it was also a symbol of impurity, lubricity.[49]

The Biblical text "Thou shalt walk upon the lion and asp and the basilisk, and Thou shalt trample under foot the lion and the dragon" (Psalm 91:13) could be easily transposed by an artist into an ornamental design of a zoomorphic triad composed of a naturalistic lion, a fantastic biped and an asp, as seen, for example, in the bas-relief in the Gniezno door border, in the right lower corner of the right wing (Figure 5).

This illustrates how, in a dialogue between the artist-creator of the work and the viewer-recipient of that work, a created visual image had the power to carry a symbolic as well as literal sense of the word.[50]

Nonetheless, the American art historian and educator Meyer Schapiro, without denying the possibility of the existence in medieval church art of imagery "designed as symbol or as illustration of a sacred text," challenged the principle that Romanesque religious art was always symbolic or illustrated a religious theme.[51] He maintained that within the framework of church art there had emerged, by the eleventh and twelfth centuries in Western Europe, a "new sphere of artistic creation without religious content," one that had not been submitted to "fixed teaching or body of doctrine" but was "imbued with values of spontaneity, individual fantasy, delight in color and movement, and the expression of feeling...This new art, on the margins of the religious work, was accompanied by a conscious taste of the spectators for the beauty of workmanship, materials, and artistic devices, apart from the religious meanings."[52]

The medieval art scholar Jurgis Baltrušaitis observed that the Romanesque artist's choice of ornamental motifs, composed of the association of plants, animals, monsters and humans, as well as the method of their application, juxtaposition and play with one another, was not the result of an accidental, spontaneous artistic improvisation, or fantasy. Based on observations of precise mathematical factors, *"sort de calcul mathématique, d'une géometrie savamment établie"* [out of mathematical calculation, of a wisely established geometry], it was the result of a complex, strictly organized, structured system.[53]

Henri Focillon's view of medieval art was that it was an "intellectual art" in which the "laws which govern the distribution and composition of its forms are themselves the products of sublime thought."[54]

Had the decorative system within the border of the Gniezno door been organized according to any laws of mathematical principles? And, was it possible that application of mathematical formulas had been used to reinforce the bond, the tension, between the ornamental context of the door's border and of the door's central imagery, portraying the dramatic life of St. Adalbert?

Presented below is a new analysis of the ornamental motifs in the Gniezno door's border; it makes an attempt to reveal the presence of several principles in the border's composition.

It shows that the specific choice of fantastic versus naturalistic fauna and flora themes, the ration of their distribution combined with the manner of their reciprocal, or interacting, association may have allowed the artist to infuse the marginal border ornamentation of each of the two door wings with decorative rhythms and aesthetic moods of quite different and contrasting natures, yet each wing's border remained harmonious with the topic of the pictorial narrative of religious meaning that unfolds vertically on that wing.

	Left wing	Right wing
Fantastic palmette-leaf blossoms:		
The *rinceau's* 43 convolutions		
enclose 8 such blossoms as their		
central fill-in motifs or	18.6%	
The 42 convolutions enclose		
32 such blossoms or		76.2%

Fantastic animal forms:
Of the total of 23 animal forms,
10 are imaginary or   43.5%
Of the total of 35 animal forms,
24 are imaginary or   68.6%
Animal forms, both naturalistic
and fantastic, crossed or lassoed
by plant forms:
Of the total of 23 animal forms,
14 are crossed by vegetation or   60.9%
Of the total of 35 animal forms,
28 are crossed by vegetation or   80.0%

These percentile figures show that the right wing *rinceau* framing that wing's central religious images of a stormy part of St. Adalbert's life, ending with his martyrdom, is inhabited by a prevalently imaginary zoomorphic world and a botanical life of abstract, schematized, pseudoplant forms of rigidly decorative palmette-leaf blossoms. There are frequent entanglements or a mutually constraining crossing, or lassoing, of animal forms by vegetative elements that transform and distort their prey's anatomical extremities into plants. Within the fantastic, abstract zoomorpho-botanical forms of the right wing *rinceau* dwell four human figures, depicted as if they were suspecting a lurking danger; they either carry weapons or are confronted by animal forms.

Among the imaginary animal forms are numerous depictions of serpentlike, reptilian monsters (thirteen, in comparison to four in the border of the left wing of the door). Their presence appears to inject into the right wing border an accelerated rhythmical order, pervading it with elements of strangeness, restlessness, and a latent menacing force combined with the sense of an underlying vigilance.

The serpentine monster, although shown in a variety of renditions, is endowed with a coiling body, canine head with a voraciously open snout, two heavy, clawed feet, and the wings of a bird. The image of that fearsome hybrid has been regarded as the classic element of a decorative vocabulary of animal-form motifs of Romanesque-era art.[55] It is said that this bizarre creature, when forming a component of the ornamental schema of an artistic work, had the power to focus the gaze and attention of the viewer by conveying to him at once a sense of horror and fascination, awe, fear and veneration.[56] Its seminal source is sought in the "serpent in the Garden of Eden...[which] gave humankind knowledge of good and evil and with it the burden of original sin."[57]

In contrast to the right wing's *rinceau* decoration, the left wing's *rinceau* projects the aesthetic mood of a rather serene, peaceable kind, remaining in accord with the atmosphere of the adjacent central religious narrative of the wing, representing a normal and tranquil phase of Adalbert's earlier saintly life.

The left *rinceau* is inhabited mainly by a botanical and animal world whose forms either replicate those found in nature or appear to have been patterned on real life. Notwithstanding their stylized decorativeness, fewer of them depict fantastic flora or fauna, and all show a lesser degree of mutual entanglements and metamorphoses.

The five human figures seen within the left wing *rinceau* are pursuing the everyday occupations of vineyard harvest, or hunt.

Such a sympathetic choice of marginal ornamental motifs, derived from the varied and exuberant world of plants, animals, monsters and humans but applied in accordance with the mathematical principle of numbers, arrangement and associated relationships, lends itself to the notion that the choice was neither an accident nor an incident, but rather was intentional and meant to achieve a structured and regulated composition for the marginal ornamentation framing the principal visual field with its religious content. Earlier in this article, a question was posed regarding the possibility of the existence of a mutual reference between the central religious theme imagery in Romanesque art and its marginal, nonreligious theme decorative element, and the extent to which that element participated in the telling of the central imagery of the artistic work.

On the basis of the analysis of the ornamental *rinceau* border in the Gniezno Cathedral's door presented here, the border appears to have been calculated to intimately relate, to unite, the world of the ornamental border with the central religious theme imagery of the door in a meaningful thematic relationship and harmony.[58] In that relationship, the marginal frame was not a "passive element." Although an ancillary element to the principal pictorial narrative, it played an enhancing, supportive role to it. Attracting and capturing the imagination and the viewers' gaze, the border's ornamental attractiveness, its vivid expression of life and the sense of "exploitation of the unexpected" helped to create and maintain the intensified visual interest between the beholder and the work of art.[59]

It is also felt that the artist's choice of the ornamental motifs in the border was aimed at helping the viewer to gain a deeper perception of the meaning of the door's central imagery, of its religious, abstract message, by sensualizing the latter, as it were, for the beholder's gaze. And, by participating in a symbolic presentation of the battle between good and evil, the marginal ornamentation of the *rinceau* border projected its engagement in a message carrying a moral point of view as well.[60]

It may be concluded that the border of the Gniezno door has been playing the role of an articulator of the message con-

✠

tained in the door's main pictorial narrative. The marginal ornament in the door's decorative schema appears to play the role of an "ultimate mediator" which, fraught with a "sensory pleasure,"[61] is—if one may use the expression of Oleg Grabar—an "unenunciated but almost necessary manner of compelling a relationship between objects or works of art and viewers or users."[62]

Further exploration of the pictorial language, and its sources, of Romanesque art ornamental motifs derived from a natural world of plants and animals, from monsters and human themes, and the attempt to gain understanding of the complex relationship between man's art and nature, leads into a combination of the areas.

One may perceive such an ornament to have been the fruit of artistic spontaneity[63] in a sensitive observer of forms, color and movement in the world of living nature,[64] within the contemporary medieval culture that was marked by a pronounced increase of interest in natural sciences and the universe.[65] (It was once remarked that the "grandeur" of a "vision of man and of his relationship with the universe is revealed to us in medieval art.")[66] The Romanesque ornamental motifs discussed here might also have been conceptualized as hidden bearers of moralizing symbolism.[67] They were compatible with the twelfth-century state of mind disposed to searching for symbolic meanings in the animal world, both natural and imaginary, [68] an inclination nourished by the medieval culture rooted in the elements of folklore and popular belief, in the survivals of myth, fable, travel accounts, astrological illustrations and encyclopedia bestiaries.[69] They also sprang from artistic expression that migrated from various interpenetrating cultures of the ancient East, Hellenistic and Roman antiquity, and Islam.[70]

Such motifs might also have had their source in man's direct experience of his environment. For the twelfth-century artists and craftsmen, the hermit monks and their lay brothers working for monastic and church patrons, that environment had been mainly a rural wilderness in an overwhelmingly agriculturally structured society. It manifested itself not only in natural beauties, in the pleasing interaction of association with animals and birds, but also in hostile powers of the world of nature and in unpredictable and menacing appearances of the animal inhabitants. In such an environment, the eremitic minds, accustomed to an isolated, self-contained, rigorously ascetic life, conceived of the artistic ideas that were inspired by the notions of God, the universe, human population, animals and plants—real and fantastic—merging in harmony in an interdependent web of life.[71]

One may also hypothesize that the motif of a convoluting vine stem inhabited by themes borrowed from the natural world might have captured the imagination of a medieval artist and of the beholders of his work as the physical embodiment of a vision of the spiritual landscape, proclaimed in Christ's words: "I am the vine, you are the branches" (John 15:5). Or it might have reminded the artist and the beholders of his work of a Biblical reference that God Himself placed man in the "vineyard," a Garden of Paradise, "to be mindful of it, and tend it" (Genesis 4: 8, 15).

One may also take into consideration the thoughts of Edward O. Wilson, a Harvard University biologist, that human beings are bound to other living things of the world by their natural affinity for life, which he described as "biophilia" and considered central to the evolution of the human mind. He defined the "biophilic instinct" as the "innate tendency to focus on life and lifelike processes," to explore and "affiliate with other forms of life."[72] Guided by this inner direction, people examine with curiosity and wonderment the natural world of animals and plants around them, often tingeing that world with magic, symbols and fantasies, often drawing moral lessons from nature by translating the agents of nature into the symbols of their culture.[73]

The elements of a growing new realistic attitude toward the surrounding world of nature, a curiosity and wish to gain knowledge of it, were especially characteristic in Europe during the second half of the twelfth century,[74] the time within which art historians are now crediting the execution of the bronze door of the Cathedral of Gniezno.[75]

Medieval notions celebrating nature are related, in a sense, to the twentieth-century deep awareness of our natural environment and major ecologically conscious concerns "faced...with the diminishing richness and vitality of life on Earth," calling for the assiduous protection of the natural environment for the present and future.[76]

Modern, turn-of-the-twentieth-century viewers of a Romanesque inhabited *rinceau* are less theological than their medieval predecessors in overlaying the meaning of plant and animal life ornamental designs with the power of Christian symbolism and allegory. Thus they are not oriented toward deciphering potential theoretical meanings of such emblems of medieval thought. They are nonetheless close to the Romanesque artists who searched for their inspiration in nature. The roots of that closeness rest in a shared "biophilic instinct," in humankind's "feeling for nature" and tendency for an intimate interaction with the natural world.

The fact that these common sensibilities exist may eventually prove to be of aid to our speculations concerning the inherent meaning of popular medieval ornament composed of motifs whose forms are evocations of the world of nature.

TABLE IV

The Plant-Form Designs on the Border of Both Wings of the Gniezno Door

The plant motif on the border of the left wing is composed predominantly of ornamental forms reflecting a synthesis of nature and decorative stylization. Some twenty-five botanical forms sprout along the vine-*rinceau*'s stem, swaying vigorously in multiple directions as if they represent a naturalistic growth.

Among these forms are clusters of grapes and mushroomlike shapes; floral symbols in the form of a round bowl or a cup, from some of which issue ornamental central spikes; small tripartite designs of two leaves symmetrically flanking a third element; meandering tendrils; and long, narrow tentacle-like forms spreading and clutching onto the stem with their tips. Among the leaflike organs are various shapes and surfaces: oblong, round, oval, longitudinal and spatulate. Some leaves, presented singly, or grouped, have plain blade surfaces, while others are veined, plastically lobed, or rendered in deep, ridged lines. Some have scalloped edges; the blades of others are evenly outlined or delicately dentated. Some foliage is shown curled up and folded over, while other leaves are unfurling in a vigorous twist. Some designs are symmetrical, while others are composites of nonsymmetrically arranged clusters.

Among the plant forms, one type of leaf design predominates, though in a variety of ramifications. It is rep-

resented by a motif of an elliptical leaf, folded longitu-
dinally, and shaped into a spoon- or scoop-like form.
The leaf's folded-over part—juxtaposed against the
plain wall of the leaf's farther side—has a radially lobed
surface, finished with a scalloped edge; the edge
extends into a little volute forming a curling tip of the
leaf, and into a spiral, developed at the base of the leaf.

This design introduces a stylistic regularity to the
botanical designs of the Gniezno door's *rinceau* in both
wings. It is a component of the foliage specimens that
appear to reflect the border's naturalistic flora, imitating
the world of nature; also it is part of the highly stylized,
fantastic forms of palmette-leaf blossom designs that—
in contrast to the naturalistic plant ornamentation of the
left wing's border—form the principal elements of the
ornamental vegetation on the border of the right wing
of the Gniezno door.

These palmette-leaf blossoms are constructed as single, large, static fill-in ornaments, inscribed within the
interior of the *rinceau 's* convolutions as their terminal
embellishments. Poised on a twig borne upon the stem
of the *rinceau* coil, the blossoms—resembling a longitudinal section of a showy, natural flower—are composed
of five elements: an ornamental projection pointing
upward in a pistil like fashion, and four petals, in symmetrically placed pairs at the sides of that central organ.
Each petal is formed of the lobed, folded-over scooplike
leaf that also appears in the naturalistic type of the
Gniezno border plant designs.

———— ✠ ————

Table V

Enumeration of the Animal- and Avian-Form Designs
Belonging to Real-World Fauna on the Border of
the Gniezno Door

In the left wing: A running dog chases a hare. A hare
flees. A bird pecks at grapes. A wounded squirrel,
pierced by an arrow, rests in a leaf. A bird, perhaps a
raven, sits on the branch and picks at the feathery
fronds of a leaf. A bearded goat, crowned with a pair of
long, straight horns, climbs a vine trellis and eats a
bunch of grapes. A wolf lopes. An antlered stag, with its
head turned back, seems to flee an unknown danger. A
rooster with a large beak perches on the leaves. A raven-
like bird strains its neck to reach down for a cluster of
grapes. A monkey grasps a scroll's stem and reaches
with its mouth for a bunch of grapes. Two single lions
with their heads turned back open their jaws to devour
the branches of a scroll; their tails, gracefully curved
along the outline of their abdomens, end in ornamental
vegetal tufts, and their round heads, with small, alert
round ears, are encircled with three fringes of curling
locks that form luxuriant manes.

In the right wing: A monkey forages in a winding stem
of the *rinceau*. A small bird plucks at a palmette leaf.
Another small bird is similarly occupied. A lion,
inscribed in the *rinceau 's* convolution, turns its head
and opens its mouth to devour a leaf. Two long-legged

waterbirds stand amid the foliage. A running dog, whose head is turned backward and tail curved under its abdomen, extends its tongue, which transforms itself into a motif of a twig and—eventually—into the stem of the *rinceau*. A little bird, perched on the stem of the *rinceau*, eats a leaf. A similar bird engages in the same activity. A crouching lion, its mouth open, seems to be biting the hand of a man sleeping nearby; its tail terminates in an ornamental tuft.

TABLE VI

Enumeration of the Imaginary-Animal Motifs
on the Border of the Gniezno Door

In the left wing: A serpent with a dog's head, its coiling body is transformed into the *rinceau's* stem. A centaur-like creature's mouth ejects a winding stem; the left hand supports the stem's offshoot, laden with a cluster of grapes, while the right hand clasps the body of the canine-headed serpent. A round "slice" of an animal face serves as the terminal motif for the *rinceau's* stem. An animal head is placed at a junction of the spiraling stem in such a manner as to make the *rinceau's* convolutions emerge from the cranium of the animal to form two powerful horns; through its open mouth thrusts a fragment of the *rinceau* stem. A dragon with a canine head and the front body of a goat, protected by armor-like wings folded on the back, has a coiled tail transformed into a leaf. The body of a human-headed quadruped twists in a knot; its hind part stretches upward, while its front bends down—the *rinceau* stem seems to enter the creature's cap-covered head, reemerging through the wide-open mouth as a vegetal cluster. Two dragons are entwined in the *rinceau's* spirals, their serpentine hind parts totally transformed into vegetative elements of the *rinceau*. Both dragons possess a pair of heavily clawed paws and have armored wings folded on their back; their long necks and open mouths strain to reach for clusters of grapes. A small leonine head resembles one of the leaves sprouting from the end of the *rinceau's* stem. A bird, a peacock perhaps, with a diadem of three pins on its head, eats grapes. The bird has a powerful neck, wings, and claws, and it trails a heavily plumed tail.

In the right wing: A monster has the body of a reptile, the head of a dog, and the wings of a bird; its body is transformed into the stem of the *rinceau*. The dragon's fanged jaws spew the *rinceau's* winding stem. A similar dragon, on two powerful, clawed feet, with a tail terminating in a tripartite vegetable design, strains its neck and opens its mouth to devour the *rinceau's* flowerette. A bird of prey is seen in flight, with its beak open and wings spread and a tail in the form of a leaf. A winged monster—part mammal, part reptile—with the rear part of its body transformed into a design of two foliate elements, is swallowing a branch of the *rinceau*. An S-shaped mammalian creature with enormous furry paws rests slung over the *rinceau* stem. It has an open snout with a protruding tongue and seems to be biting its own back. Its tail twines into a convolution of the *rinceau*, filled with the motif of a palmette blossom. A winged biped, with two powerful furry forelegs, terminates in the vegetal elements of the *rinceau*. The dragon's long, coiling neck carries a canine head adorned with shaggy beard. A mammalian beast is designed in a circular out-line; the neck and head are tucked between the forelegs and extend under the abdomen. The beast's open jaws attack its own tail. A birdlike dragon has a serpentine, coiling tail at the end of which is a vegetative tuft; the creature nibbles at a palmette blossom. Yet another mammal has a tail terminating in foliate growth; it stretches its canine head on a long neck to reach with open mouth for the scroll's branch. A strange beast with a canine head and big feline forepaws has hind parts in the shape of a coiling, serpentine tail. The beast's mouth is wide open, and the protruding tongue assumes the form of a vegetal motif.

A group of three beasts seethe with ferocity at one another as if ready to attack. A lion with a round head wears a fine mane of five rows of curls. The lion's head is turned backward. The mouth spouts an S-shaped band, which appears to form the lion's tongue but sub-sequently becomes the tail of a serpent, the canine head of which confronts the lion. The lion's tail serves as the linking element between the lion and the third beast of this closely intertwined zoomorphic group—a winged biped: part bird, part dog, part reptile. The monster's fanged jaws form the cavity through which a long stem of the *rinceau* is passing. A galloping centaur that has its head turned back; his arms stretch to grasp the vegetal stem. A dragon with an earless, bald canine head, long neck, powerful forelegs and claws, has a legless coiled-up rump; the creature appears to be eating one of the *rinceau's* twigs, which, in a fanciful transformation, adopts the form of the beast's own protruding tongue. A doglike figure samples an offshoot of the *rinceau*. A mammal nibbles at a bunch of grapes; the monster's long tail, terminating in foliate ornamentation, loops gracefully under the belly of the animal before it loops again over the *rinceau* stem. A winged biped with a canine head and a reptilian body strains its long neck to bite a branch. The branch looks as if it were the beast's own protruding tongue. The monster had serpentine hind parts. A winged biped has a human head. The face is bearded. The head is covered with a headdress consisting of a round cap with two flying ribbons at the back. The creature (a siren) has a serpentine tail, knotted at its end in such a manner as to form a figure eight; the monster turns back its head and nibbles at the palmette-leaf blossom. A centaur blows a horn. A biped with the head of a dog, two heavy forelegs, and a legless rear, coils and transforms into rich vegetal elements of the *rinceau*. It strains its long neck to bite a twig of the *rinceau* stem. A mammalian creature with an enormous neck coiled into a circle opens its snout to spit out a foliate motif. The tail of this quadruped terminates in a bowlike vegetal form. The stumpy, big paws are clawed. The head is adorned with a ruff of sideburns and a shaggy beard at the throat. A coiled serpent with a canine head and open jaws emerges from the thicket of the *rinceau's* foliage. An imaginary quadruped, heavily muscled, humpbacked, and with leonine hindquarters and powerful clawed paws, has a huge neck and head with the beak of a bird of prey. A small dragon opens its fanged mouth with a tuft of flying hair at the throat. The beast possesses one pair of legs only—at the front; the rest of the body is shaped into a long tail, which—after coiling once—changes itself into the vegetal ornamentation of the *rinceau*.

TABLE VII

Enumeration of the Human-Figure Motifs
on the Border of the Gniezno Door

In the left wing: A naked figure of a man posed astride the twisting stem of the vine-*rinceau*. The man, wearing a helmetlike cap, blows a horn. A similar figure sits astride a stem laden with clusters of grapes and other plant forms; this figure is an archer, who draws the arrow to his bow and takes aim. Another man, clothed in a short tunic, stands among various vegetal forms laden with clusters of grapes; his arms are slightly raised as if he were at work in a vineyard. A fourth man, clad in a tunic, sits astride the stem of the *rinceau*; he carries on his back a bucket filled with grapes, and his left hand holds a bunch of grapes, while the right hand brings to his mouth one grape to sample. Yet another man is occupied with winemaking; while his raised arms clasp a stem laden with grapes, his feet trample the grapes in a small tub.

In the right wing: A man armed with a sword confronts a monster—part bird, part dog, part reptile. A second man, wearing a short tunic, lifts a round shield and a sword; he faces two long-legged birds in a bush. A naked human figure, asleep in a semi-reclining position, is approached by a lion whose open mouth seems ready to engulf his arm. Another naked person, stretched astride a vining stem, cuts the stem of a bunch of grapes with a knife.

NOTES: CHAPTER TWO

1 Jan Zachwatowicz, *"Architektura"* [The Architecture], *Katedra gnieźnieńska*, Vol. 1, chap. 1, p. 12.

2 Zachwatowicz, chap. 1, pp. 14-21, 23-31, 37; chap. 2, pp. 37-39.

Zachwatowicz and others, *Katedra gnieźnieńska*, vol. 1, p. 187.

In Poland, where Christianity was adopted in 966, the Cathedral of Gniezno has always been regarded as the first church in the hierarchy of Polish churches, occupying an important place in its national life. The Gniezno archbishops held the title of Primate of Poland and were empowered to rule the country during *interregna*. The cathedral functioned as a coronation church of the old monarchy. It was also the site of privilege for burials of distinguished individuals and of members of prominent Polish families.

Zygmunt Świechowski, *"Gotycka katedra gnieźnieńska na tle współczesnej architektury europejskiej"* [The Gothic Cathedral of Gniezno on the Background of Contemporary European Architecture], *Katedra gnieźnieńska*, Vol. 1, pp. 60-61.

Jadwiga Irena Daniec, Review of *Katedra gnieźnieńska* [The Gniezno Cathedral], by Jan Zachwatowicz and others, Aleksandra Świechowska ed., *The Polish Review*, vol. 17, no. 3, (1972), pp. 94-100.

3 Kalinowski, *"Treści ideowe i estetyczne drzwi gnieźnieńskich,"* *Drzwi gnieźnieńskie*, Vol. 2, pp. 7, 9.

Zachwatowicz, *"Architektura,"* chap. 1, pp. 30-31.

The Gniezno door's origin is unknown. It is regarded as a work of art of the last tier, or the last quarter, of the twelfth century (probably its eighth decade), but that dating has not yet been definitively decided. See Zachwatowicz and others,

Katedra gnieźnieńska , Vol. 1, p. 188; also Morelowski, who dates the door to "about 1170" in *"Drzwi gnieźnieńskie, ich związki ze sztuką obcą a problem rodzimości,"* p. 66; and Walicki, *"Dekoracja architektury i jej wystrój artystyczny,"* p. 229. The door was presumably cast on Polish soil by foreign, or foreign and native, craftsmen, itinerant artists of that era. See Walicki, p. 229, and Morelowski, *"Drzwi gnieźnieńskie, ich związki ze sztuką obcą...,"* pp. 53, 55-56, 58-59, 72, 75, and 99.

The epigraphical-paleographical analysis of the door's surface performed in 1955 revealed the remnants of lettering (engraved with a hammered chisel) at the base of the door knocker of the left wing. Also traces of signatures are distinguishable on the left molding of the left wing. The visible part of the lettering at the knocker's base is assumed to conceal the cipher of someone whose name was *Petrus* (or *Piotr* in Polish).

The inscriptions along the left molding of the left wing show only two words in Latin that are legible, reading *ME FECIT* [I have been made by]. The rest of the inscriptions may be deciphered hypothetically only. See Budkowa and Wolff, *"Napis na listwie drzwi gnieźnieńskich...,"* pp. 387-390; Gieysztor, *"O napisach na drzwiach gnieźnieńskich,"* pp. 415-418; Kalinowski, *"O nowo odkrytych inskrypcjach,"* p. 394, 402, 405-406; Walicki, p. 229; Maria Pietrusińska and Gieysztor, Walicki and Zachwatowicz, *Katalog i bibliografia zabytków* [Catalogue and Bibliography of Monuments], *Sztuka polska przedromańska i romańska do schyłku XIII wieku*, Vol. 2, p. 690; and Stanisław Wiliński, *"Nad monogramem drzwi gnieźnieńskich"* [On the Monogram of the Gniezno Door], *Drzwi gnieźnieńskie*, Vol. 1, pp. 101, 111-116; Zachwatowicz and others, p. 191.

The door is rectangular in shape. It consists of two wings of somewhat different dimensions. The left wing is approximately 10 feet 9 inches high by 2 feet 9 inches wide, while the right wing's height measures about 10 feet 7 inches and its width 2 feet 8 inches. The wings' thickness varies from 0.59 to 0.98 inches. See Tadeusz Dziekoński and Kornel Wesołowski, *"Charakterystyka metaloznawczo-technologiczna drzwi gnieźnieńskich"* [The Metalographic-Technological Characteristics of the Gniezno Door], *Drzwi gnieźnieńskie*, Vol. 1, p. 125; Morelowski, *"Drzwi gnieźnieńskie, ich związki ze sztuką obcą...,"* p. 43; Pietrusińska and others, p. 690; Zachwatowicz and others, p. 188.

X-ray photography of the door points to a likelihood that the left wing might have been cast in one piece, or perhaps in a few large pieces; the right wing consists of twenty-four small parts which, in all probability, were soldered together after being cast separately. Each of the wings bears traces of damage—in the form of cracks along the almost entire height, leading from its knockers upward and downward—that was subsequently repaired. See Dziekoński and Wesołowski, pp. 125-126, 129, 135-139, 142-145, 147, 150-151, 155, 161, 182; Pietrusińska and others, p. 690; Zachwatowicz and others, p. 188. The surfaces of both wings show traces of round bronze pegs that penetrate the relief side to the reverse. Their heads are flattened and leveled off flush with the surface of the wing, and they had been used to fasten the bronze ornamental surface to its backing of wood. Seven singly spaced pegs were placed in various areas of the relief panels of the left wing; seventeen, arranged in pairs (except one) in the upper corners of each panel, held the panels of the right wing. See Dzickoński and Wesołowski, pp. 126-127, 137, 153-155, 163; and Zachwatowicz and others, p. 188.

4   See Jadwiga Karwasińska, *"Rozwój legendy o Św. Wojciechu"* [A Development of the Legend of St. *Wojciech*], *Drzwi gnieźnieńskie*, Vol. 1, pp. 20-41; see also Jacopo da Voragine, *Złota Legenda* [The Golden Legend], translated from the Latin editions of *Legenda Aurea* (Theodor Graesse

[Dresden-Leipzig, 1846, first edition], and Anton Koburger [Copinger No. 6429, Nürnberg, 1482]), by Janina Pleziowa (Warsaw: Pax, 1955), pp. 208-209, 211-226; Tadeusz Wojciechowski, *Szkice historyczne jedenastego wieku* [Historical Sketches of the Eleventh Century] (Cracow: Państwowy Instytut Wydawniczy, 1951), pp. 33-37, 47, 80-82, 103, 305; also Thomas Carlyle, History of Friedrich II of Prussia, called Frederick the Great (London: Chapman and Hall, 1873, ten volumes), Vol. 1, pp. 56, 80.

5 Maguire, "The Art of Comparing in Byzantium," pp. 88-89, 91, 93-94, 98, 102.

6 *Drzwi gnieźnieńskie*, Vol. III: *Album. Dokumentacja Fotograficzna* [Album. Photographic Documentation], illustrations 1-87.

Goldschmidt, *Die Bronzetüren von Novgorod und Gnesen*, illustrations II/71-II/101.

Kalinowski, *"Treści ideowe i estetyczne...,"* pp. 14-54.

Karwasińska, pp. 20-26.

Łapiński, pp. 95, 100-101, maintains that chronology of the events in St. Adalbert's life represented on the Gniezno door differs from that reported by the historical sources.

Walicki, *"Dekoracja architektury...,"* p. 229.

Walicki and others, *Sztuka polska przedromańska i romańska...*, Vol. 1, illustrations 1175-1184.

Pietrusińska and others, p. 690.

Zachwatowicz and others, Vol. 1, pp. 189-191; Vol 2, illustrations 121-129.

7 One of the most famous such pilgrimages was made in 1000 by the German Holy Roman Emperor Otto III, an ardent promoter of the development of the cult of St. Adalbert in Europe. Under Otto's patronage, Gniezno, previously subordinated to the Diocese of Magdeburg, was to become an independent ecclesiastical province in Poland. See Aleksandra Świechowska and Zygmunt Świechowski,

"Konfesje Św. Wojciecha" [The Sepulchers of St. Adalbert], *Katedra gnieźnieńska* , Vol. 1, pp. 126-128; Zachwatowicz and others, Vol. 1, pp. 16, 23-24, 457; *Mistrza Wincentego kronika polska* [Poland's Chronicle by Master Vincent], translated by Kazimierz Abgarowicz and Brygida Kürbis, with preamble and commentaries by Brygida Kürbis (Warsaw: Państwowe Wydawnictwo Naukowe, 1974), p. 103.

8 Dziekoński and Wesołowski, p. 125.

9 A narrow molding embellished with straight lines, convex and concave, placed parallel to the door's edges, frames the border on the top, bottom and outer (hinged) sides. The right wing of the door is suspended on four hinges, one of which is a later replacement. Originally, the left wing had five hinges. The top one is the only hinge remaining. (See Dziekoński and Wesołowski, pp. 125 and 127). For an exhaustive study of the ornamental border of the Gniezno door, see in particular Kalinowski, *"Treści ideowe i estetyczne..."* pp. 56-115, and Zdzisław Kępiński, *"Symbolika drzwi gnieźnieńskich"* [Symbolism of the Gniezno Door], *Drzwi gnieźnieńskie,* Vol. 2, pp. 161-283; also Daniec, "The Bronze Door of the Gniezno Cathedral in Poland," *The Polish Review,* vol. 11, no. 4 (1966), pp. 10-65; and Daniec, The Gniezno Door and Its Border (unpublished Master of Arts thesis, Faculty of Philosophy, Columbia University, in the Avery Art/Architecture Library, New York City, 1965), pp. 1-334, illustrations 1-85.

10 Jalabert, pp. 68 and 98.

11 Jalabert, pp. 11 and 67.

12 André Grabar and Carl Nordenfalk, *Romanesque Painting* (New York: Éditions d'Art Albert Skira, 1958), p. 153.

13 Kauffmann, pp. 19, 26-28, describes the development of foliage from "fleshy" (derived from Anglo-Saxon decora-

tion) to a thinner type, with spirals more regularly and tightly wound, that occurred about 1170, introduced from France.
Jalabert, pp. 57 and 75.
Grabar and Nordenfalk, pp. 174-177.

14 Grabar and Nordenfalk, pp. 153 and 181.

15 The expression borrowed from Linda Seidel, "Anomalous Carving in Romanesque Sculpture: Accident, Incident or Intention?," Program Sessions, College Art Association Annual Conference (Houston, 1988), p. 7.

16 Oleg Grabar, *The Mediation of Ornament*, The A.W. Mellon Lectures in the Fine Arts, 1989 (Bollingen Series; vol. 35, no. 38), The National Gallery of Art, Washington, D.C. (Princeton, New Jersey: Princeton University Press, 1992), p. 202.

17 Grabar, pp. 202 and 210.

18 Kauffmann, p. 26.

19 Schapiro, "On the Aesthetic Attitude in Romanesque Art," p. 6.

Bennett D. Hill, *English Cistercian Monasteries and Their Patrons in the Twelfth Century* (Urbana, Chicago, London: University of Illinois Press, 1968), pp. 6 and 12.

Kalinowski, *"Treści ideowe i estetyczne...,"* p. 121.

Dom Jean Leclerq O.S.B., *"Aspects littéraires de l'oeuvre de Saint Bernard"* [Literary Aspects of the Work of Saint Bernard], *Cahiers de civilisation médiévale Xe-XIIe siècles*, vol. 1, no. 4 (1958), pp. 425-450.

Zarnecki, *The Monastic Achievement* (New York: The McGraw-Hill Book Company, 1972), pp. 71-74.

Conrad Rudolph, *The "Things of Greater Importance," Bernard of Clairvaux's Apologia and the Medieval Attitude Toward Art* (Philadelphia: University of Pennsylvania Press, 1990), pp. 7, 112, 116, 120, 124, 171, 261. See also pp. 11-12 and 283 for the translation from Latin of an excerpt from the letter written by St. Bernard about 1124-1125 to his friend the

Venerable Father William, abbot of Saint-Thierry, *Apologia ad Guillelmum Abbatem* [A Justification to Abbot William]. For the full Latin text, see Rudolph, pp. 232-287, as well as J.P. Migne, editor, *"Apologia ad Guillelmum." Patrologiae Cursus Completus* (Petit-Montrogue: 1854), vol. 182, chap. 12, par. 29, p. 915:

...what is that ridiculous monstrosity doing, an amazing kind of deformed beauty and yet a beautiful deformity? What are the filthy apes doing there? The fierce lions? The monstrous centaurs? The creatures, part man and part beast? The striped tigers? The fighting soldiers? The hunters blowing horns? You may see many bodies under one head, and conversely many heads on one body. On one side the tail of a serpent is seen on a quadruped, on the other side the head of a quadruped is on the body of a fish. Over there an animal has a horse for the front half and a goat for the back; here a creature which is horned in front is equine behind. In short, everywhere so plentiful and astonishing a variety of contradictory forms is seen that one would rather read in the marble than in books, and spend the whole day wondering at every single one of them than in meditating on the law of God. Good God! If one is not ashamed of the absurdity, why is one not at least troubled at the expense?

Schapiro in "On the Aesthetic Attitude...," pp. 6, 11, remarked that the "whole of this letter calls for a careful study; every sentence is charged with meanings that open up perspectives of the Romanesque world."

20 Erwin Panofsky, *"Suger, opat St. Denis"* [Suger, the Abbot of St. Denis], *Studia z historii sztuki* [Studies from Art History], edited by Jan Białostocki (Warsaw: Państwowy Instytut Wydawniczy, 1971), pp. 66, 77, 82-94.

Schapiro, "On the Aesthetic Attitude...," pp. 7-8, 14.

Rudolph, pp. 104-105, 108, 111.

21 Focillon, pp. 102 and 105.

✠

Ernst H. Gombrich, *The Sense of Order. A Study in the Psychology of Decorative Art* (Ithaca, New York: Cornell University Press, 1979), pp. 255-256.

22 Kalinowski, "*Treści ideowe i estetyczne...*," p. 123. For the presentation of the author's hypotheses, see pp. 7-146.

Kępiński, p. 260.

Mossakowski, "*Drzwi gnieźnieńskie a kronika polska Mistrza Wincentego,*" pp. 27 and 35.

23 Kalinowski, "*Treści ideowe i estetyczne...*," pp. 113, 121, 130.

Kępiński, pp. 163-166, 185, 254, 260, 268-270. For the total presentation of the author's arguments, see pp. 161-283.

24 Kępiński, pp. 164, 260, 269.

Kalinowski, "*Treści ideowe i estetyczne...*," pp. 124 and 130.

Mossakowski, "*Drzwi gnieźnieńskie a kronika polska...*," p. 27.

25 Mossakowski, "*Drzwi gnieźnieńskie a kronika polska...*," pp. 20 and 26.

26 J.L. Schrader, "A Medieval Bestiary," *The Metropolitan Museum of Art Bulletin*, 1986 (Summer), p. 3.

27 Schrader, pp. 3, 5-9; see also Louis Réau, *Iconographie de L'Art Chrétien* [The Iconography of Christian Art] (Paris: Presses Universitaires de France, 1955), Vol. 1, pp. 59-61, 64-65, 76-77; and T. H. White, *The Book of Beasts, Being a Translation from a Latin Bestiary of the Twelfth Century* (New York: Dover Publications, Inc., 1984), pp. 231-237, 243-246. Among the important works of the twelfth and thirteenth centuries illustrating the common views of the era, see the commentaries: *Speculum Naturale* by Vincent de Beauvais; *Speculum Ecclesiae* by Honorius d'Autun; *De Bestiis et aliis rebus*, ascribed to Hugh of Saint Victor; *Mitrale* by Sicardo, the Bishop of Cremona; *Aviarium-Bestiarius* by Hugo de Folieto; or *Rationale divinorum officiorum* by Guillaume

Durand, the Bishop of Mende. Certain elements of medieval animal symbolism had roots in the Bible, mainly in the Psalms; others reached back to prehistoric times, passed on by oral tradition, as well as the writings of Greek and Roman historians and philosophers (Herodotus, Aristotle, Plutarch, or Pliny the Elder). Most medieval observations and descriptions of animals are found in the so-called Latin bestiaries, works of natural history, written and illustrated in the monasteries. Their purpose was both interpretative, summarizing a contemporary knowledge of the world of animals and their habits and traits, and didactic, imbued with their moralizing significance through description of human traits in animal behavior. These pseudo scientific treatises included zoological accuracy and fables, myths and fabulous creatures, based on the Greek work by an anonymous author known as Physiologus and also on the Elder Pliny's *Historia Naturalis*, a Roman encyclopedia of the physical world of the first century AD.

28 Schrader, p. 5.

Réau, pp. 60-61, 63. Saint Thomas of Aquinas (1225-1274) formulated the essence of medieval thought as "Christocentric," that neither humanity within the frame of its history, nor the world of nature had any meaning in themselves, but were meaningful only insofar as they led the way toward Christ (*in quantum ducunt ad Christum*). Everything was regarded as emanating from God and gravitating toward Him. In this context, the animal world, both natural and under the guise of imaginary forms, was interpreted as Christologically symbolic.

29 Réau, pp. 61, 63, 78.

Lynn White Jr., "Natural Science and Naturalistic Art in the Middle Ages," *American Historical Review*, vol. 52, no. 3 (April 1947), pp. 424-425.

30 The formulation based on Erwin Panofsky, pp. 80-81.

31 Schrader, pp. 3-7.

✠

Réau, pp. 76-78.

32 Réau, p. 132.

Schrader, p. 3.

Kalinowski, "Treści ideowe i estetyczne...," p. 128.

33 Réau, p. 76.

Schrader, p. 6.

"Animals as Symbol in Medieval Illuminated Manuscripts," Exhibition at The Pierpont Morgan Library, New York City, *In the Company of Animals*, a City-Wide Collaborative Program Exploring the Relationship of Animals and Humans, sponsored by the New School for Social Research in cooperation with The Asia Society, The Pierpont Morgan Library, The Museum for African Art, The Academy of American Poets, The Jewish Museum, 1995 (March 31-December 31).

34 Réau, pp. 76 and 65.

35 Réau, p. 63.

Schrader, pp. 3-4.

36 Gieysztor, *"Drzwi gnieźnieńskie jako wyraz polskiej świadomości narodowościowej w XII wieku"* [The Gniezno Door as an Expression of Polish National Consciousness in the 12th Century], *Drzwi gnieźnieńskie*, Vol. 1, p. 5.

Mossakowski, *"Drzwi gnieźnieńskie a kronika polska...,"* pp. 30 and 36. See also Huizinga, p. 213.

37 Arnold Hauser, *The Philosophy of Art History* (New York: Alfred A. Knopf, 1959), p. 48; see also Réau, pp. 59-60.

38 Hauser, pp. 49, 102, who said: "Ambiguity may originate in the most varied circumstances, but it is above all, a result of a latent meaning prevented, for some reason or other, from expressing itself directly. Its artistic attraction consists in the presence of an unknown, unrealized, but none the less most effective, factor of an impenetrable and therefore apparently inexhaustible source of excitement."

39 Kalinowski, *"Treści ideowe i estetyczne...,"* p. 97.

Réau, pp. 92 and 110. The lion motif is symbolically ambivalent, as it could also be understood as a personification of Satan.

Schrader, pp. 4 and 12.

T.H. White, pp. 7-9.

40 Mroczko, p. 32.

Gieysztor, *"Przed portalem płockiej katedry,"* p. 9; it personified "undoubtedly the sign of Hell."

Kalinowski, *"Treści ideowe i estetyczne...,"* p. 97.

Réau, p. 92; *"tantôt comme l'incarnation du Démon"* [sometime as the incarnation of the Devil].

41 Kalinowski, *"Treści ideowe i estetyczne...,"* pp. 100-101.

Réau, pp. 83-84, 88, 102, 105, 129-130.

Schrader, p. 36.

T.H. White, p. 151.

42 Schrader, pp. 26 and 33.

Gieysztor, *"Przed portalem...,"* p. 9.

Kalinowski, *"Treści ideowe i estetyczne...,"* p. 104.

Réau, pp. 101, 109, 118-119, 129.

T.H. White, pp. 61 and 64.

43 Réau, p. 130.

Kalinowski, *"Treści ideowe i estetyczne...,"* p. 96.

Schrader, p. 25.

T.H. White, pp. 56, 59.

44 Schrader, p. 24.

Réau, p. 114.

T.H. White, p. 51.

45 Schrader, p. 46.

Réau, p. 114.

Kalinowski, *"Treści ideowe i estetyczne...,"* pp. 97, 107.

46 Kalinowski, *"Treści ideowe i estetyczne...,"* p. 96.

Réau, p. 82.

T.H. White, p. 37.

47 Réau, pp. 111-112.

✠

Kalinowski, *"Treści ideowe i estetyczne...,"* p. 101.

48 Kalinowski, *"Treści ideowe i estetyczne...,"* p. 104.

Schrader, p. 40.

49 Schrader, pp. 21, 43-44, 47.

Kalinowski, *"Treści ideowe i estetyczne...,"* p. 6.

Réau, pp. 112-113, 115-116, 129, 131.

T.H. White, pp. 34, 74, 142, 167.

50 Schapiro, *Words and Pictures. On the Literal and the Symbolic in the Illustration of a Text* (Mouton, The Hague, Paris: 1973), pp. 9, 13-14, 18.

Mieczysław Gębarowicz, *"Niektóre zagadnienia metodologii historii sztuki"* [Some Problems Regarding the Methodology of Art History], *Biuletyn Historii Sztuki*, vol. 38, no. 2 (1976), part 1, pp. 138-139, 146, 148.

Kępiński, p. 271.

Réau, pp. 340, 389.

51 Schapiro, "The Bowman and the Bird on the Ruthwell Cross and Other Works...," p. 351.

Schapiro, "On the Aesthetic Attitude...," pp. 1-3, 5-6, 10.

Kalinowski, *"Treści ideowe i estetyczne...,"* p. 121.

Kępiński, pp. 165, 260.

52 Schapiro, "On the Aesthetic Attitude...," pp. 1-2, 5, 10.

Réau, p. 65.

53 Jurgis Baltrušaitis, *"La stylistique ornamentale dans la sculpture romane"* [The Ornamental Style in Romanesque Sculpture], *Études d'art et d'archéologie publiées sous la direction d'Henri Focillon* [Studies of Art and Archaeology Published Under the Direction of Henri Focillon] (Paris: Librairie Ernest Leroux, 1931), pp. 66, 69, 98, 101, 106, 144, 151-152, 161. See also a critique of Baltrušaitis' idea of an "underlying ordered scheme" in Romanesque art in Meyer Schapiro, "On Geometrical Schematism in Romanesque Art," *Romanesque Art*, pp. 266-268.

54 Focillon, p. 8.

55 André Grabar and Carl Nordenfalk, *Early Medieval Painting* (Lausanne: Éditions d'Art Albert Skira, 1957), p. 177.

56 Edward O. Wilson, *Biophilia* (Cambridge, Massachusetts, and London: Harvard University Press, 1984). pp. 83-86, 101, 106. See also Kępiński, p. 164; and Gombrich, p. 256: these hybrid creatures "seen as representations of 'real' monsters...inspire fear of the unknown and the demonic; seen as playful inventions they make us laugh."

57 Wilson, p. 100; see Genesis 2:14.

58 Walicki, "*Dekoracja architektury...*," p. 229.

59 Gombrich, p. 276.

60 Kalinowski, "*Treści ideowe i estetyczne...*, p. 130.

Kępiński, p. 270.

Even though one ought to distinguish symbolic figures from purely decorative ones: see Réau, pp. 64-65; and also Schapiro, "On the Aesthetic Attitude...," p. 10, and "The Bowman and the Bird...," p. 351.

61 Oleg Grabar, pp. 37, 231, 237, notes that by providing pleasure, ornament gives to the observer the right and freedom to choose meanings. Kalinowski, "*Treści ideowe i estetyczne...*," p. 122, speaks of a secondary type of symbolism borne in the mind of the viewer independently of the one envisaged by the artist-creator.

"Pleasure through the eyes," said Margaret Olin, in a review of Oleg Grabar's "The Mediation of Ornament," in *Art Bulletin*, vol. 75, no. 4 (December 1993), p. 730.

62 Oleg Grabar, pp. 45, 230, 237.

63 Schapiro, "On the Aesthetic Attitude...," pp. 1, 10.

64 Schapiro, "On the Aesthetic Attutide...," pp. 10-11.

65 Kalinowski, *Treści ideowe i estetyczne...*," pp. 141-142.

Kürbis, "*Polska wersja humanizmu średniowiecznego u progu XIII wieku*" [A Polish Version of Medieval Humanism at the Onset of the 13th Century], *Sztuka i ideologia XIII wieku*

✠

[Art and Ideology in the 13th Century], edited by Piotr Skubiszewski (Wrocław, Warsaw: Polska Akademia Nauk, Ossolineum, 1974), pp. 12, 16.

66 Focillon, p. 7.

67 Kalinowski, "*Treści ideowe i estetyczne...*," p. 123.

Kępiński, pp. 163, 254.

68 Kępiński, pp. 163, 165-283.

Kalinowski, "*Treści ideowe i estetyczne...*," pp. 88-115 and 124.

Mossakowski, "*Drzwi gnieźnieńskie a kronika polska...*," p. 27.

Réau, p. 76.

69 Schapiro, "On the Aesthetic Attitude...," pp. 10 and 22.

Kalinowski, "*Treści ideowe i estetyczne...*," pp. 108-113.

70 Kalinowski, "*Treści ideowe i estetyczne...*," pp. 108-113.

Kauffmann, p. 26.

Kępiński, pp. 272-274, 276-277.

Focillon, p. 115.

Gombrich, pp. 256, 271.

Schapiro, On the Aesthetic Attitude...," pp. 16 and 20.

71 Schapiro, "On the Aesthetic Attitude...," p. 7

Paul Piehler, *The Visionary Landscape, a Study in Medieval Allegory* (Montreal: McGill-Queen's University Press, 1971), pp. 72-73, 78-79, 84.

Hill, pp. 1-8, 10-11.

72 Wilson, pp. 1, 22, 85, 139-140.

73 Wilson, pp. 10, 85-86, 97.

74 Dobrowolski, p. 101.

Kalinowski, "*Treści ideowe i estetyczne...*," pp. 140-142.

Gieysztor, "*Drzwi gnieźnieńskie jako wyraz...*," p. 17.

Lynn White Jr., pp. 421-422, 424-425, 434-435.

75 Gieysztor, "*Drzwi gnieźnieńskie jako wyraz...*," pp. 1, 8, 12.

76 Suzi Gablik, "The Ecological Imperative," *Art Journal*, vol. 51, no. 2 (Summer 1992), p. 51; and Thomas Berry, "Art in the Ecozoic Era," *Art Journal*, vol. 51, no 2 (Summer 1992), pp. 46-48.

CHAPTER THREE

An Enigma: The Medieval Bronze Church Door of Płock in the Cathedral of Novgorod

On November 23, 1981, and February 28, 1982, two jubilant celebrations were held at Płock in Poland, in the presence of representatives of the Polish government, the Polish church hierarchy, the artistic community, and the public at large. The ceremonies marked the welcoming, placement, and consecration of an ornamental bronze door in the main portal of the Cathedral of Płock. The bronze door is an exact copy of the church door that is today set in the western portal of the façade of the Orthodox Cathedral of *Sancta Sophia* in Novgorod in Russia (Figure 7).[1]

The majority of Polish sources argue that the unique twelfth-century Romanesque door in Novgorod was originally intended not for the Cathedral of *Sancta Sophia* but for the Cathedral of Płock, where it had been initially installed, and that the door was eventually moved from the site at Płock to Novgorod.[2] The circumstances and the time of the move remain undocumented.[3]

In Poland, proposals to return the door from Novgorod to the Cathedral of Płock, its presumed original medieval site, had been put forth on various occasions, but with no success.[4] In 1970, during the Thirteenth International Congress of Historical Sciences, held in Moscow, a new plan was introduced by the chairman of the Płock Scientific Society, Dr. Jakub Chojnacki. He suggested that a bronze copy of the door in Novgorod be executed and then installed at the Cathedral of Płock.[5] This unusual proposal, supported by the government of Poland, received the official seal of approval of the Ministry of Culture of the then Soviet Union, and permission was granted for Polish specialists to begin a bronze recast of the original door at *Sancta Sophia*. The execution of the project (backed financially by the government of Poland and the Mazovian Petrochemical Refineries of Płock) lasted eleven years.[6]

Thus the door—regarded in Poland as a priceless monument of its culture,[7] and estimated[8] to have hung at the entrance to the Płock Cathedral some 830 years ago—is now rehung in that same spot in the form of its bronze copy. The measurements of the recast exactly match the frame of the cathedral's original Romanesque entrance.[9] The door is suspended on newly provided hooks,[10] whose position corresponds to the placement of medieval iron hooks, of which four out of the original total of eight remain intact in the jambs of the Płock Cathedral's portal.[11] (The extant four hooks, discovered by the Polish architect Stefan Szyller during the renovation of the cathedral in 1903, were identified by him as the authentic twelfth-century ones. Szyller estimated that the hooks had served to support a heavy Romanesque door.)[12]

Several hypotheses exist to explain when and how the door reached Novgorod. Theories about the time the door was moved range anywhere from the tenth through the fifteenth centuries, and historians are uncertain whether it was sent to Novgorod as a gift, an object of sale or, perhaps, according to a Novgorodian-transmitted belief cited in Russian literature, a trophy of war, a *"voennye trofei."*[13] The idea that the door was a war trophy (regarded by some historians as the only plausible explanation) is not generally accepted by Polish sources.[14] Rather, the majority doubt it, favoring a theory proposed in the 1850s by the illustrious Polish historian Joachim Lelewel. He hypothesized that the door was a gift presented to the city of Novgorod. He also suggested that this presentation must have occurred either in the fifteenth century or at the end of the fourteenth.[15]

Although Lelewel's observations are still rejected by some Polish sources,[16] they eventually found support in an epigraphic analysis (1970s) by the Polish scholar Andrzej Poppe of some sixty words in the Cyrillic alphabet[17] that—along with the twenty-four inscriptions in twelfth-century Latin[18]—are engraved on the bronze surface of the door. The analysis revealed that the syntax and orthography of the Cyrillic inscriptions are characteristic of established usage between the years 1439 and 1450.[19]

Since, in all likelihood, the inscriptions were executed after the door's arrival in Novgorod, as originally proposed by Lelewel,[20] Poppe's linguistic analysis led to the currently held opinion that the door from the Cathedral of Płock was placed in the façade of *Sancta Sophia* Cathedral sometime between the years 1439 and 1450.[21]

This position has the advantage of jibing with other historical facts. One of these, for example, is the fact that the Archbishop of Novgorod, Euthemius II, is known to have undertaken in the years between 1439 and 1450 important restorative and decorative work on the Cathedral of *Sancta Sophia*. (Much of the church had been destroyed in the fourteenth century, especially by fire in 1340).[22] Euthemius's plans for the cathedral, conjectures Poppe,[23] might have included the acquisition of an ornamental bronze door. Also, it should be borne in mind that dynastic connections within the multinational Polish-Lithuanian-Ruthenian territories of the day might have played a facilitating role in arranging for the presentation of the door as a gift to the Cathedral of Novgorod. Władysław Jagiełło, a Lithuanian duke by birth, became Poland's king (1386-1434) and the founder of its Jagiellonian dynasty. The influences of a Lithuanian-Ruthenian tie at the Polish Jagiellonian court were described as pronounced.[24]

Jagiełło's marriage to Jadwiga of Anjou, the hereditary successor to the crown of Roman Catholic Poland, resulted in the union of Poland and Lithuania, as well as in the official introduction of Catholicism into Lithuania in 1387. But the vast Ruthenian lands grouped around the Lithuanian nucleus were inhabited by an Orthodox population, gravitating toward the Orthodox Great Russian State of Moscow. Simultaneous to all of this were new plans aimed at a religious union between the Orthodox and Catholic churches.[25] It was Lelewel[26] who first advanced the theory that Simon Lingwen, then the Prince and Governor of Novgorod (and one of the brothers of Władysław Jagiełło and Alexandra, the wife of Ziemowit IV [1382-1424], the Prince of Płock), obtained the cathedral door from the ecclesiastical community of Płock and, in about 1400, donated it to the cathedral in Novgorod. It may have been a gesture in which art, politics, the church and secular powers combined to make a statement of rapprochement between the Latin church's community of Płock and the Orthodox Novgorod.

The inscriptions on the Novgorod door's decorative bronze panel-fields identify, amid the other imagery, the three figures of the artist-craftsmen who made the door (the bottom row of the left wing). The inscriptions proclaim that these individuals were named Riquin, Waismut (Vvaismuth) and Avraam.[27]

In addition, the artists immortalized themselves in solemn-looking self-portraits, rendered in bronze bas-relief. Such self-portraits are a "major surprise" on any of works of art of that era, said Aleksander Gieysztor, a Polish historian.[28]

The Novgorod door makers are depicted carrying the tools of their trade. Over the tall man, wearing richly patterned clothing of below-the-knee length, a Latin inscription—announcing *"Riquin me fec"* (Riquin made me)—indicates that Riquin was the principal master (Figure 8). His face is that of an older man, bearded and mustachioed; his hair is a round-shaped skullcap of concentric ridges. In his right hand he holds a pair of scales, while a pair of tongs rests on his left shoulder. Riquin's companion and assistant, Waismut (Figure 9), with clean-shaven face and shoulder-length hair parted in the middle, is smaller and younger than Riquin, and clothed more modestly. The tongs and a long, pointed burin are clasped in both his hands. The third craftsman (Figure 10), identified as Avraam (or Abraham), is pictured with three instruments: the tongs, a hammer, and a ladle for pouring liquid metal. Like Riquin, Avraam appears to be an older man, bearded with a mustache and a skullcap coiffure. He is dressed similarly to Riquin, but, in contrast to Riquin and Waismut, whose shoes reach only to their ankles, Avraam is shod in higher, midcalf boots.

The figures of Riquin and Waismut are identified by both Latin and Cyrillic inscriptions. In contrast, Avraam is identified by only a fifteenth-century Cyrillic inscription. There has been a long-standing dispute among scholars over the identity of Avraam. To some historians he is a figure of the Romanesque era.[29] But other, quite opposite views hold that Avraam's portrait is a later addition to the door's decorative schema, an addition that actually belongs to the Novgorod phase, and represents a self-portrait of the master craftsman who was responsible for reassembling the wings of the door after its arrival at Novgorod.[30]

The execution of the Novgorod door is also connected to two church dignitaries, historically documented individuals of twelfth-century Europe; and their portrait representations, like those of the door's artist-craftsmen, appear on the door in bas-relief. The engraved inscriptions establish the identity of these two churchmen (bearing crosiers and raising the index and middle fingers of their right hands in a gesture of blessing or *allocutio*), as the bishops *"Vicmannus Megideburgesis Epc"* and *"Alexander Epc De Blucich."*[31] Alexander (Figure 11) is shown being assisted by two deacons (left wing, the plate below the door pull), with his name recorded in both Latin and Cyrillic, in contrast to Vicmannus (right wing, in the middle of the second row from the bottom of the door), identified solely in Latin (Figure 12).

The bishops' diocesan seats denote, respectively, the German city of Magdeburg and the Polish town of Płock, rendered here in corrupted medieval Latin, according to Friedrich von Adelung, the first scholar to solve the puzzle of the words *De Blucich*.[32]

Historians (starting with Lelewel) credit the origin of the Novgorod door to the artistic patronage of Alexander, the Bishop of Płock between the years 1129 and 1156. A native of Malonne, near Namur and west of Liège (in present-day Belgium), the bishop became a distinguished patron of art and architecture and played a dominant role in making Płock an important cultural center in Poland (other cultural centers of the time were Cracow and Gniezno). In his capacity as bishop, Alexander is known to have begun construction of the city's cathedral, consecrated in 1144. It is conjectured that it was for that cathedral that Alexander commissioned an ornamental bronze door to be cast in Magdeburg (the site of the archdiocese upon which the Płock bishopric had been dependent prior to 1136).[33]

Historical sources state that Vicmannus directed the archdiocese of Magdeburg as its archbishop (*archiepiscopus*) from 1154 to 1192, after having first served there as bishop (*episcopus*) between the years 1152 and 1154.[34] Since the inscription on the door identifies Vicmannus as *"episcopus,"* art historians have narrowed the date of the Płock-Novgorod

✠

door's origin to the years between 1152 and 1154 (Adolph Goldschmidt, a German scholar, was the first one to do so).[35]

The inclusion of the portraits of both Alexander and Vicmannus in the door's decoration led to the assumption that a link must have existed between them during the period of the door's commission and execution. However, there is no documentation to confirm the role played by either bishop in initiating the execution of the door. Were they (or was one of them) the door's patron? Was perhaps one priest the donor, endowing the other with the gift of the door? Was Bishop Alexander the actual initiator and principal patron of the door, who having commissioned it at Magdeburg desired to commemorate Vicmannus, then the Bishop of Magdeburg? Or was Bishop Vicmannus himself either a founder of the door or an intermediary?[36]

There are some historians who emphasize the importance of Bishop Vicmannus in commissioning the door.[37] This point of view, it is said, can be supported by the fact that the door's decoration includes not only portraits of the two bishops but also likenesses of the artist-craftsmen, the makers of the door. The purpose of such inclusion might have aimed at advertising Magdeburg (which toward the middle of the twelfth century had become an important center for the casting of bronze) by calling attention to the local artists creating in that medium.[38] And the Magdeburg artists who made the door might have included a portrait of Vicmannus in order to pay homage to the bishop of their city's diocesan seat.[39]

One may regard the questions relating to the identity of the commissioning patron of the Płock-Novgorod door as the dominant ones in the study of that door. But important too are the questions that seek to define the role of the patron, as well as his connection to the artist-craftsmen who executed the door. For although throughout the Middle Ages, "conceptualization and execution of works of art were largely independent,"[40] it has been noted that the patronage of a commissioned medieval art "often involved an explicit and subtle interaction between adviser and artist."[41] Patrons were not only instigators of medieval art projects but also planners, providers of material for these projects, formulators of their content, and learned advisers, while the realization of the project remained the imaginative work of artists.[42]

It would have been much more practical for the Bishop of Magdeburg, rather than the far-off Bishop of Płock, to have sponsored and supervised the creation of a work of art being executed at a local Magdeburg workshop. Nonetheless, Kazimierz Askanas,[43] a historian of Płock's cultural heritage, tends to exclude the possibility of Bishop Vicmannus's patronage in commissioning this particular door. Askanas points to the fact that Vicmannus is portrayed within the iconographic program of the door as the person of lesser rank; that is to say, his figure is smaller than the figure of Bishop Alexander, and unlike Alexander, he is represented without the assisting deacons. But historians do state[44] that Vicmannus (Wichmann), named to the bishopric and archbishopric of Magdeburg by King Frederick I Barbarossa, the Holy Roman Emperor (1152-1190), was an enormously influential and powerful churchman. He is said to have rendered "invaluable services" as an adroit diplomat and adviser to Frederick I,[45] whose foreign policies also included an interest in the Slav territories east of the River Elbe.[46]

These facts allow one to speculate—in contrast to the view held by Askanas—that the fashioning of a smaller-size portrait of Vicmannus for the door may have been a purposefully calculated and politically astute act on the part of the Bishop Vicmannus, known for a carefully planned program of expanding his diocese of Magdeburg by promoting both commerce and colonization east of the Elbe.[47]

✠

Marian Morelowski, an eminent Polish art historian, postulated that it was Vicmannus who commissioned the door for Bishop Alexander,[48] an outstanding churchman as well as a knight (described by the Polish medieval chronicler Wincenty Kadłubek as *"agnus et lupus"*) and a mighty protector of Poland's province of Mazovia, with the purpose of gaining Alexander's support for his (Vicmannus's) agenda of political and ecclesiastical change.[49]

One can further postulate that Vicmannus wanted a sign of symbolic modesty to minimize his own importance in the gift he was offering: he chose to emphasize the person of Bishop Alexander, for whose cathedral the gift was intended, by directing that the latter's likeness be more important and larger in size than his own. Alexander's importance, it is further observed, was also significantly stressed in the door's decoration by the gesture of one of the deacons accompanying him. The deacon, standing on the right side of Alexander, extends his arm and points his forefinger toward Alexander.

In examining the Płock-Novgorod door's decorative schema[50] (Table VIII), we see two wings subdivided into twenty-six compartments (thirteen in each wing). Twenty-four of these compartments, or panel-fields, placed in horizontal pairs, are almost square; the two uppermost ones, crowning the door's wings, are in the form of rectangles, measuring double the width of the square compartments below them. The subdivision is achieved by thick, semicircular bronze moldings, placed vertically and horizontally across the face of each wing and along its sides. They are embellished with a dense vegetal pattern of boldly drawn, winding and interweaving stylized stems, foliage, and flower forms, sculpted in relief and marked with linear engravings. At the points of their intersection, the moldings are affixed to the door's wooden underbase by means of rivets with ornamental four-petal heads. Within the moldings are plates of bronze bearing figural imagery cast in bas-relief. The plates are framed and held in place not only by these moldings; they are also additionally reinforced and secured to the door's underbase by narrow borders of flat strips of bronze, patterned with a series of floret-shaped nail heads and a modest vegetal and geometric design.

TABLE VIII

The Schema of the Płock-Novgorod Door's Imagery

The left wing	The right wing
The enthroned Christ, accompanied by the Sts. Peter and Paul, the Virgin Mary and a group of the twelve Apostles	Christ in majesty; two dragons under his feet; his mandorla supported by the four angels and surrounded by the symbols of the four Evangelists
The baptism of Christ; The Annunciation; The Nativity; A male figure holding a book; The adoration of the three Magi; A figure with a musical instrument; Mary and the child Jesus, accompanied by an angel; Rachel bewailing her children	A male figure holding in front of him a shieldlike apron; Entry to Jerusalem; A warrior aiming his sword at a crouching lion; A male figure with a scroll; A gate to the city of Jerusalem—a procession of palms
The presentation at the temple; A deacon, with a maniple on his left arm, holding a censer; A door pull in the shape of a lion's head (five small human heads emerge	A man holding a small animal; The betrayal of Christ by Judas; A male figure holding a cane and standing upon the feet of another figure, depicted in the

from the lion's mouth)

The Visitation; The Flight to Egypt; A deacon holding a book; Bishop Alexander, accompanied by a subdeacon and a deacon, one holding a cup, the other a scroll

The prophet Elias in a fiery chariot; A group of four warriors (two victorious and two vanquished)

The master Riquin holding the scales and tongs; The temptation: Adam and Eve; The master Avraam (Abraham) holding the tongs, hammer, and a ladle; The creation of Eve; The master Waismut holding the tongs and burin

upside-down position and holding a scroll; A man with a snake coiled about his body; St. Peter in chains, accompanied by guards carrying swords

A door pull in the shape of a lion's head (a human head emerges from the lion's mouth); A crowned man holding a short sword; A man with a spear confronting a crouching beast; A tiny figure with clasped hands; Herod, crowned, and enthroned, and holding a scepter and sword; The scourging of Christ

The Crucifixion; A man holding an oil vessel; A (Ruthenian?) dignitary; The women at the sepulcher

Christ's descent into hell; Bishop Vicmannus of Magdeburg; The Ascension; A man with a sword and a scabbard

Three knights treading a dragon (including, perhaps, St. Maurice? [a patron saint of the diocese of Magdeburg]); The massacre of the innocents; The centaur

The imagery depicted on the door's panel-fields includes human and zoomorphic forms as well as some architectural, arboreal, and plant elements. The main themes comprise interpretations of Old and New Testament subjects, mixed with representations that do not specifically pertain to religion (Figure 13).

The New Testament themes depict twenty-one subjects: the baptism of Christ, the Annunciation, the Nativity, the adoration of the Magi, the Virgin Mary and the Child with an angel, the presentation at the temple, the Visitation, the flight to Egypt, entry into Jerusalem, a procession of palms, the betrayal of Christ by Judas, St. Peter in chains accompanied by guards carrying swords, Herod enthroned, the scourging of Christ, the Crucifixion, the women at the sepulcher, Christ's descent into hell, the Ascension, the massacre of the innocents.

The uppermost part of the left wing shows the enthroned Christ, assisted by Sts. Peter and Paul, and surrounded by a group including the Virgin Mary and the twelve Apostles. In the uppermost part of the right wing, there is Christ in majesty within a mandorla, supported by four angels and surrounded by the symbols of the four Evangelists.

The four images based on the Old Testament are Rachel bewailing her children, the prophet Elias in a fiery chariot, the temptation in the Garden, the creation of Eve.

The door's other images depict a variety of men; some clothed in ecclesiastical garb, some clad in armor. There are two groups of warriors, as well as two single individuals carrying swords, a crowned personage, and a man with a musical instrument. Other figures are engaged in symbolic confrontation with animals (a lion, a monster); one man holds a small animal; another stands with a snake coiled about his body. Three of the men are carrying scrolls; two have books; others are holding a censer, an oil vessel, a cup, a cane, or a shieldlike apron. The remaining two figures carry no identifying attributes. Finally at the bottom of the right wing, in its right corner, there is a figure of ancient Greek legend, the centaur, half man and half horse. Two bronze door pulls, sculpted in the form of humanoid-lionesque masks holding tiny human heads in their jaws—five heads in the left door pull and one in the right—complete the decorative schema of the door.

The relief work in which the images on the door are molded is executed on a flat, spaceless setting of bronze plates. The height of the relief is graded. It varies from fully plastic forms that project from the bronze background (at times even disengaging themselves from their metallic wall, as in the areas of heads and limbs), to forms that move gradually closer to the background as the sculpturing descends to the body's trunk. The relief work has been described as "aggressive" and of an "expressive character," drawn with an "almost brutal force."[51] The relief is defined by rather stiff shapes and hard-edged outlines, and drawn within the area of the body and vestments with sharply engraved lines. Human figures are most often presented frontally, and most of them appear rather massive looking. Their characteristic feature is a large head sculptured almost in the round and placed close to the torso, nearly neckless. A well-modeled, abundantly fleshy face—bearded or beardless—has an expressively molded mouth, large bulging eyes, and a long, prominent nose with a sharp ridge delineating the nose's bridge. The hair is usually combed in the form of a skullcap, parted in the middle. Sometimes it falls to the shoulders in ridged strands.

In some instances the imagery is not confined exclusively to the areas of the door's bronze plates. In six places it invades, as it were, the area of the large convex moldings

that frame the plates: in four places, segments of the moldings are actually nonexistent, having been replaced by sculptured figural forms; in the remaining two cases, small
human figures are depicted emerging from the moldings'
vegetal surface decoration.

In the ornamental imagery of the Płock-Novgorod door,
some Polish scholars claim to see a clearly presented principal idea. Rudziński[52] describes it as the "history of salvation." Świechowski[53] reads it as the "salvation cycle, from the
scene of the creation of the first man to the enthroned Christ
as the Judge in his heavenly splendour, surrounded by the
symbols of the Evangelists," with the "motif of a victorious
fight against evil" playing a very important part in the context of the door's decoration. Chojnacki[54] calls the door one
of the "heaviest catechisms" in the world, considering its
weight (2,400 kg, or 5,290 lbs.) and size (360 cm by 240 cm,
or 11 feet 8 inches by 7 feet 9 inches).

In contrast, other Polish sources (Gieysztor, Walicki and
Knapiński, for example) argue that the didactic essence of
the principal pictorial program of the door is not easily com-
prehended. The existing mixture of religious and secular
images has been assembled in many instances without any
chronology or apparent thematic coherence. This fact dims
the clarity of the ideological theme of the door's iconographic program.[55]

The present conjectural reading and interpretation of the
Płock-Novgorod door leads one to suspect that its current
pictorial composition is probably rather different from its
original, twelfth-century version, whose scenario was not
preserved and remains lost to the modern viewer.[56]

Herbert Kessler of Johns Hopkins University observed
that in medieval times works of art were apt to be continu-
ously reused, remounted, and integrated within new settings

over long spans of time, to be assimilated, "recycled,"[57] as it were, into new programs of ornamentation. Medieval objects of art "were often the product of an accretive process, compiled rather than fashioned."[58]

On the basis of Kessler's remarks, one may speculate that the program of ornamentation now existing on the Płock-Novgorod door is the result of just such a process of accretion and recycling. This proposition is supported by the existence in the door's decorative program of an agglomerate of representations of sacred and secular episodes and symbols, forming no continuous pictorial narration, but rather functioning as independent images; the motivation of their selection and placement is difficult to read.

Another argument in support of the accretive, or recycled, character of the Płock-Novgorod door's decoration is based on the manner in which the forty-eight plates bearing their sculpted imagery are fitted into the twenty-six panel-fields of the door, enclosed within the framework of the convex ornamental moldings subdividing the surface of the door.

While only six of these panel-fields contain a single square plate decorated with sculpted image (such plates were cast separately and later assembled to form the decoration of the door),[59] the remaining twenty panel-fields accommodate two or even three separate, individual, rectangular-shaped plates with images. Each plate bears the image generally unrelated in subject to its fellows within the same area of a panel-field.

The placement of more than one pictorial plate within the door's panel-field gives the impression of these plates being artificially cut to size and assembled in order to fit precisely into the available inner area of the door's panel-fields. Such placement highlights the presence of their unevenly shaped forms, indicating some irregularity of line and "primitive incisions"[60] at the joining edges of the plates.

One may pose a question: Have, perhaps, some of the original Magdeburg-executed decorative bronze plates been mixed with possible later replacements[61] for the Płock-Novgorod door that might at one time have constituted the components of a different work of art? Or were some of the pictorial plates executed afresh, in order to be mounted, fitted, and fused along with the original Magdeburg-executed plates into a new decorative entity: an ornamental door destined for the monumental architectonic decorative system of the Cathedral of *Sancta Sophia*?

In conclusion, as Poppe also suggests,[62] it will take a chemical analysis of the components of the bronze alloy from which the individual decorative plates were made to shed light on the enigma of the Płock-Novgorod door.

✠

✠

NOTES: CHAPTER THREE

1 Jakub Chojnacki, *"Drzwi płockie zawisły w bazylice katedralnej 23 listopada 1981 roku"* [The Door of Płock, Suspended in the Cathedral Basilica on November 23, 1981], *Romańskie drzwi płockie, 1154—ok. 1430-1982*, pp. 117-124.

Chojnacki, *"Romańskie drzwi płockie—idea kopii i jej realizacja"* [A Romanesque Płock Door—the Idea and the Realization of Its Copy], *Romańskie drzwi płockie*, pp. 75-81.

The Rev. Wacław Gapiński, *"Uroczystość przekazania i poświęcenia kopii romańskich drzwi płockich w bazylice katedralnej w Płocku"* [The Ceremony of Conveyance and Consecration of the Copy of the Romanesque Door of Płock in the Cathedral Basilica in Płock], *Romańskie drzwi płockie*, pp. 51-70.

Bogdan Sikorski, the Bishop of Płock; a speech given at the Cathedral of Płock on February 28, 1982, *Romańskie drzwi płockie*, pp. 65-66.

2 Askanas, *Sztuka płocka*, pp. 54-61. He also cites the contrasting views of Feliks Zygmunt Weremiej in *"Śladami zagubionych ogniw"* [Tracing the Lost Links] (Warsaw, 1977), pp. 55-65, who doubts the door ever reached Płock; and the views of Hans Joachim Krause and Ernst Schubert in *Die Bronzetür der Sophien Kathedrale in Novgorod* [The Sophian Cathedral's Bronze Door in Novgorod] (Leipzig, 1968), p. 47, who refrain from offering any hypotheses relating to the manner in which the door reached Novgorod. For extensive bibliographical listings on the subject of the Płock door, see Askanas, *Sztuka płocka*, pp. 361-393.

Askanas, *Brązowe drzwi płockie w Nowogrodzie Wielkim*, pp. 9, 19-21, 27-37. For lists of extended bibliography, see also pp. 47-50.

Chojnacki, *"Romańskie drzwi płockie—idea kopii...,"* p. 73. He credits (along with Askanas) Joachim Lelewel, a nineteenth-century Polish historian, with introducing into Polish scholarship the concept of this door as the "Płock door."

Andrzej Poppe, *"Z nowszych badań nad drzwiami płockimi"* [From the Recent Inquiries Into the Door of Płock], *Romańskie drzwi płockie*, pp. 30 and 38.

Świechowski, p. 67.

Walicki, *"Dekoracja architektury i jej wystrój artystyczny,"* p. 228. According to him, there is no certainty that the present Novgorod door was ever incorporated into the façade of the Cathedral of Płock.

Płock, situated on the Vistula River northwest of Warsaw, is a modern industrial center. It is also one of the oldest cities in Poland. Placed along an important trade and cultural-currents route between the West and East, it functioned between 1079 and 1138 as the capital of the country, and afterward as the seat of the Mazovian and Płock princes. Two medieval Polish kings, Władysław I Herman (1079-1102) and Bolesław III Krzywousty (1102-1138), are buried in the Cathedral of Płock. Dating back to the first half of the twelfth century, the cathedral served as the bishopric seat of the Diocese of Płock. See also the following:

Askanas, *Sztuka płocka*, pp. 13-19.

Chojnacki, *"O drzwiach płockich—streszczenie"* [About the Płock Door—Summary], *Romańskie drzwi płockie*, p. 132.

Chojnacki, *"Romańskie drzwi płockie—idea kopii...,"* p. 70.

Pietrusińska and others, *Katalog i biblioteka zabytków*, p. 742.

Novgorod, on the Volchov River, north of the Lake of Ilmen, is southeast of St. Petersburg. It was one of the most

✠ important centers of medieval Rus'—politically, militarily and culturally. A city-fortress, located advantageously on the East-West trade routes leading from the Baltic Sea to the Black Sea and farther, Novgorod grew wealthy from the tenth through the twelfth centuries dealing with merchants of the medieval league of the Hanse Germanic towns. The Cathedral of Novgorod, dedicated to *Sancta Sophia* (the Holy Wisdom), dates back to the years 1045-1050. See: Chojnacki, *"Romańskie drzwi płockie—idea kopii...,"* p. 81. Omeljan Pritsak and John S. Reshetar Jr., "Ukraine and the Dialectics of Nation-Building," *From Kievan Rus' to Modern Ukraine: Formation of the Ukrainian Nation.* The Millennium Series, Harvard University (Cambridge, Massachusetts: Ukrainian Studies Fund, 1984). p. 12.

3 Askanas, *Sztuka płocka,* p. 55.

Askanas, *Brązowe drzwi płockie...,*p. 28.

Poppe, p. 33.

Pietrusińska and others, p. 744.

4 Chojnacki, *"O drzwiach płockich—streszczenie,"* p. 133.

5 Askanas, *Sztuka płocka,* pp. 61-62.

Chojnacki, *"Drzwi płockie zawisły...,"* p. 117.

Chojnacki, *"Romańskie drzwi płockie—idea kopii...,"* p. 75.

Poppe, p. 30.

6 Chojnacki, *"Drzwi płockie zawisły...,"* p. 117.

Chojnacki, *"O drzwiach płockich—streszczenie,"* pp. 133-135.

7 Chojnacki, *"Romańskie drzwi płockie—idea kopii...,"* pp. 74-75 and 82. Quotes Michał Walicki in *"Ofiara złota"* [An Offering of Gold], *Arkady* (January 1939), pp. 26-27. See also Gapiński, p. 64, citing Aleksander Gieysztor as saying, "The door of Płock is a great happening in the culture of Poland..."

8 Chojnacki, *"Romańskie drzwi płockie—idea kopii...,"* p. 73.

Poppe, p. 38.

9 Askanas, *Sztuka płocka,* p. 54.

Chojnacki, *"Drzwi płockie zawisty...,"* pp. 120-121.

10 Askanas, *Sztuka płocka*, p. 54.

Chojnacki, *"Drzwi płockie zawisły...,"* p. 119.

11 Chojnacki, *"Drzwi płockie zawisły...,"* p. 121.

12 Askanas, *Sztuka płocka*, p. 54. He cites Stefan Szyller's *"O architekturze płockiej"* [About the Architecture of Płock], *Księga pamiątkowa mariańska* [A Marian Commemorative Book], (Lwów: 1905, second edition), Vol. 1, pp. 227-290.

Askanas, *Brązowe drzwi płockie w Nowogrodzie Wielkim*, pp. 21-22.

13 Goldschmidt, *Die Bronzetüren von Novgorod und Gnesen*, p. 7.

Askanas, *Sztuka płocka*, p. 56.

A legend dating from the fifteenth century connects the door with the prince of a medieval state of the Kievan-Rus', Vladimir, whose baptism in the year 988 was responsible for opening the way to Christianity. It has even been suggested that it was Vladimir who brought the door to Novgorod, as a trophy of his military expedition in 989 to Cherson, a city-port on the Dnieper River near the Black Sea. See Askanas, *Sztuka płocka*, p. 57. He mentions Friedrich von Adelung, a member of the St. Petersburg Academy of Sciences and the author of *Die Korsunischen Türen in der Kathedralkirche zur Heiligen Sophia in Novgorod* [The Korsun Doors in the Cathedral of Saint Sophia in Novgorod] (Berlin: 1823), pp. 23-26, who had referred to the door as the Cherson [Korsun] door. See also Mikhail Tsapenko, editor, *Early Russian Architecture* (Moscow: Progress Publishers, 1969), pp. 34 and 38. He refers to the door as the Kherson, or Sigtuna, door, a twelfth-century work from Magdeburg. See also Poppe, p. 34.

Still another hypothesis (introduced in the seventeenth century by Martinus Aschaneus of Sweden) assigns the door's provenance to Sigtuna, an early capital of Sweden, suggesting that the door was plundered there by the

Novgorodians, who brought it to their city in 1187. See Askanas, *Sztuka płocka*, pp. 56-57, and *Brązowe drzwi płockie...*, pp. 10, 29-35; Dobrowolski, *"Rzeźba,"* p. 105. He argues that 1170 was the year of the door's arrival in Novgorod; see also Poppe, pp. 30, 34 and 38.

One modern hypothesis (Aleksander Gieysztor and Kazimierz Askanas, for example) proposes that the door arrived in Novgorod much later, in the second half of the thirteenth century (1262). According to this theory, it was carried away from Płock by Lithuanian invaders (in alliance with the Prince of Novgorod, Alexander of Neva, 1220-1263) and subsequently either presented by them to their allies the Novgorodians, or sold to the merchants of the city of Novgorod. See Askanas, *Sztuka płocka*, p. 58, and *Brązowe drzwi płockie...*, pp. 35-37; Chojnacki, *"Romańskie drzwi płockie— idea kopii...,"* p. 71; and Świechowski, p. 67; also Morelowski, *"Drzwi gnieźnieńskie, ich związki ze sztuką obcą...,"* p. 95.

14 Chojnacki, *"Romańskie drzwi płockie—idea kopii...,"* p. 71.

15 Chojnacki, *"Romańskie drzwi płockie—idea kopii...,"* p. 71.

Chojnacki, *"O drzwiach płockich—streszczenie,"* p. 136. He cites Lelewel's opinion which is also discussed by Askanas in *Sztuka płocka*, p. 55.

Walicki, *"Dekoracja architektury i jej wystrój artystyczny,"* p. 228 (he said, "before 1340").

16 Askanas, *Sztuka płocka*, pp. 55-56.

17 Askanas, *Sztuka płocka*, pp. 58-59.

Chojnacki, *"Romańskie drzwi płockie—idea kopii...,"* p. 71.

Chojnacki, *"O drzwiach płockich—streszczenie,"* pp. 136-137.

Poppe, pp. 33-34.

18 Askanas, *Sztuka płocka*, p. 52.

Poppe, p. 32.

Pietrusińska and others, p. 744. See the paleographic analyses of the Latin inscriptions by Władysław Semkowicz in *Paleologia łacińska* [Latin Paleography] (Kraków: 1951), p. 250, which state that they are contemporary with the twelfth-century execution of the door and that they comprise two categories: first, those inscriptions (totaling eighteen) that were executed at the same time as the door's sculpted images, and were therefore subject to the bronze-casting process; and, second, the remaining six inscriptions that were additionally engraved later, after the original bronze-casting process was already completed.

19 Askanas, *Sztuka płocka*, p. 59.

Poppe, pp. 33-34.

20 Askanas, *Brązowe drzwi płockie...*,p. 13. He points out differences in the Cyrillic inscriptions and suggests they were probably executed by other artisans at different times.

Chojnacki, *"O drzwiach płockich—streszczenie,"* p. 136; and by the same author, *"Romańskie drzwi płockie—idea kopii...,"* p. 71.

Poppe, p. 33.

Walicki, *"Dekoracja architektury i jej wystrój artystyczny,"* p. 228, Pietrusińska and others, p. 744.

21 Poppe, p. 34.

Chojnacki, *"Romańskie drzwi płockie—idea kopii...,"* p. 72.

22 Askanas, *Sztuka płocka*, p. 59.

23 Poppe, p. 34.

24 Francis Dvornik, *The Slavs in European History and Civilization* (New Brunswick, New Jersey: Rutgers Universtiy Press, 1962), pp. 222-229.

Tadeusz Mańkowski, *Orient w polskiej kulturze artystycznej* [The Orient in Polish Artistic Culture] (Wrocław-Kraków: Ossolineum, 1959), p. 191. See also Adam Zamoyski, *The Polish Way* (New York, Toronto: Franklin Watts, 1988), pp. 43-44, 46, 48, 70; and *"Władysław Jagiełło,"* *Encyklopedia powszechna* [General Encyclopedia], edited by S. Olgerbrand (Warsaw: S. Olgerbrand and Sons), Vol.7 (1900)

✠

p. 129, and Vol. 15 (1903), p. 394. King Jagiełło's fourth wife, the mother of his two sons (the future Polish kings Władysław III Warneńczyk, 1434-1444; and Kazimierz IV Jagiellończyk, 1447-1492, who also bore the title of the Grand Duke of Lithuania, 1440-1492), was a Ruthenian princess, Sophia of Holszany.

25 Oscar Halecki, *A History of Poland* (New York: Roy Publishers, 1943), pp. 67-72, 74, 83-85.

26 Askanas, *Sztuka płocka*, p. 55.

Askanas, *Brązowe drzwi płockie...*, pp. 28-29.

Chojnacki, *"Romańskie drzwi płockie—idea kopii...,"* p. 71.

27 Askanas, *Brązowe drzi płockie...*, p. 15; Figure 13.

Dobrowolski, p. 105.

Gieysztor, *"Przed portalem płockiej katedry,"* p. 10.

Świechowski, p. 67; Figures 190-191.

Pietrusińska and others, p. 744.

Ulrich von Thieme and Felix Becker, *Allgemeines Lexikon der Bildenden Künstler von der Antike bis zur Gegenwart* [A General Dictionary of Plastic Artists From Antiquity to the Present Time] (Leipzig: Verlag von E.A. Seemann), Vol. 2 (1908), p. 286; Vol. 33 (1934), p. 377; and Vol. 35 (1942), p. 62.

Walicki, *"Dekoracja architektury i jej wystrój artystyczny,"* p. 227; Plates 1144-1164.

28 Gieysztor, *"Przed portalem płockiej katedry,"* p. 10.

One may add that this is not the first known instance of such portraiture rendered on a twelfth-century artwork connected with Poland. There is also a later example in Poland of an artist's self-portrait depicted on the work of art he created. It exists on a paten (dated to 1193-1202), preserved at Ląd, at the Cistercian Abbey Church of the Blessed Virgin Mary and St. Nicholas. The paten (silver gilt, engraved and niello work), was created by Conradus, a goldsmith at the court of the Polish ruler Mieszko the Old. Conradus's self-portrait and his name are wrought on the surface of the paten beneath the images he engraved and the inscriptions reading *Dux Mesico, Sanctus Nicolaus* (St. Nicholas, the patron of the Abbey of Ląd) and *Abbas Symon* (the abbey's abbot). Walicki remarked that Conradus must have felt a considerable sense of his own dignity as an artist, since he did not hesitate to place a self-portrait at the feet of St. Nicholas. For description and photographs of the paten, see Michał Walicki, *"Wyposażenie artystyczne dworu i kościoła"* [The Artistic Endowment of the court and of the Church], *Sztuka polska przedromańska i romańska do schyłku XIII wieku*, Vol. 1, part 5, pp. 279-280, 613-614; Pietrusińska and others, p. 725; Kalinowski, *"O nowo odkrytych inskrypcjach na drzwiach gnieźnieńskich,"* *Drzwi gnieźnieńskie*, vol. 2, p. 409.

29 Gieysztor, *"Przed portalem płockiej katedry,"* p. 10.

30 Askanas, *Sztuka płocka*, pp. 50-51. He mentions Russian researchers who believe that Avraam (active at the end of the thirteenth and the beginning of the fourteenth centuries) reassembled the door in Novgorod and then added his self-portrait. To make room for the portrait, Avraam cut out a fragment of the door's ornamental molding and replaced it with the sculptured image of himself. (The fact that the Cyrillic inscriptions on the door are characteristic of a later time, between the years 1439 and 1450, does not negate the role played by Avraam in an earlier reassembling of the door.)

Askanas, *Brązowe drzwi płockie...*, pp. 36-37. The author dates Avraam to the fourteenth century. He credits him with renovating the door in Novgorod, in about the year 1340.

Dobrowolski, p. 105. He regards Avraam as the restorer of the door after its transferal to Novgorod.

Pietrusińska and others, p. 744. See Joachim Lelewel's opinion regarding the role played by Avraam; it was he who assembled and completed the decoration of the door and added his self-portrait.

Goldschmidt, *Die Bronzetüren von Novgorod und Gnesen,* p. 8.

Poppe, p. 35. He questions whether Avraam was a Novgorodian.

The Rev. Romuald Rudziński, *"Historia zbawienia na drzwiach płockich"* [History of the Salvation on the Płock Door], *Romańskie drzwi płockie,* pp. 40-41. He maintains that Avraam was a Ruthenian master.

Świechowski, p. 265. He believes that Avraam may have been a Novgorod master who was responsible for the assembly of the door and the supplementation of its missing parts.

Walicki, *"Dekoracja architektury i jej wystrój artystyczny,"* p. 228.

31 Władysław Abraham, *Organizacja kościoła w Polsce do połowy wieku XII* [The Church Organization in Poland Until the Mid-Twelfth Century] (Poznań: Pallottinum, 1962), p. 198.

Askanas, *Sztuka płocka,* p. 52.

Askanas, *Brązowe drzwi płockie...,* pp. 13-14; Figures 9-10.

Chojnacki, *"Romańskie drzwi płockie—idea kopii...,"* p. 70.

Mieczysław Gębarowicz, *"Aleksander biskup płocki"* [Alexander, the Bishop of Płock], *Polski Słownik Biograficzny* [Polish Biographical Dictionary] (Kraków: Polska Akademia Umiejętności), Vol. 1 (1921), pp. 65-66.

Peter Munz, *Frederick Barbarossa, A Study in Medieval Politics* (Ithaca and London: Cornell University Press, 1969), pp. 56-57.

Poppe, p. 32.

Rudziński, p. 45.

Świechowski, p. 67; Plates 189-192.

Walicki, *"Dekoracja architektury i jej wystrój artystyczny,"* p. 228; Figures 1171, 1174; Pietrusińska and others, p. 744.

Mistrza Wincentego kronika polska, pp. 43-44, 70.

32 Von Adelung concluded that the word "Blucich" was an example of the frequent disfigurements and transformations that occurred in the spelling and writing of medieval Latin names. He believed that "Blucich" undoubtedly represented a deformed version of the name Płock. That name had been referred to in other medieval records as "Plotzke," "Urbs Plocensis," "de Ploceke," and "Plotzik." The fact that on the Novgorod door the word "Blucich" begins with the letter "B" instead of the letter "P" ("Plucich") illustrated the then interchangeable application of voiced and voiceless consonants. For example, the word "Egiptum" (for Egypt) is spelled "Egibtum" in the inscription on the Novgorod door, in the scene depicting the flight to Egypt, placed adjacent to the portrait of Bishop Alexander. See Askanas, *Sztuka płocka*, p. 52, and *Brązowe drzwi płockie...*, p. 14; also Poppe, p. 38. See also Pietrusińska and others, p. 744 (who stated that both Friedrich von Adelung and Joachim Lelewel were the first scholars to identify the bishops represented in the bas-relief portraits on the Novgorod door); in addition, see Walicki and others, *Sztuka polska przedromańska i romańska...*, Vol. 1, Illustrations 1168 and 1174.

33 Askanas, *Sztuka płocka*, pp. 17-19, 25, 30, 36, 45-46, 50, 52.

Askanas, *Brązowe drzwi płockie...*, pp. 9-10, 26. Although the Magdeburg provenance of the Płock-Novgorod door has been generally accepted, there also exist unconvincing attempts to connect the door's production with the milieu of Płock (pp. 43-44). Askanas links the Płock-Novgorod door (illustrations 1 21, 23-24) to the door in the Basilica of *San Zeno Maggiore* in Verona; he also cites the views of Russian scholars who link the door to the bronze church doors of the cathedrals of Amalfi, Ravello and Salerno, suggesting the possibility of its execution in Italy (pp. 38 and 42).

Dobrowolski, pp. 105-106 and 118.

Gębarowicz, "*Aleksander biskup płocki*," p. 65.

✠

Robert Kunkel, *"Katedra płocka w średniowieczu"* [The Cathedral of Płock in the Middle Ages], *Biuletyn Historii Sztuki*, no. 3 (Warsaw, 1988), pp. 194-197.

Poppe, p. 33.

Rudziński, p. 46.

Świechowski, pp. 23, 67, 265.

Pietrusińska and others, p. 744.

34 Askanas, *Sztuka płocka*, p. 53.

Askanas, *Brązowe drzwi płockie...*, p. 18.

Gieysztor, *"Przed portalem płockiej katedry,"* p. 10.

Goldschmidt, *Die Bronzetüren von Novgorod und Gnesen*, p. 8.

Munz, p. 56. He cites, among other sources, J. Hartung, *Die Territorialpolitik der Magdeburger Erzbischöfe Wichmann, Ludolf und Albrecht, 1152-1232* [The Territorial Policies of the Magdeburg Archbishops Wichmann, Ludolf and Albrecht, 1152-1232] (Magdeburg: Geschichtsbläter für Stadt und Land, Jahrgang 21 [1886]), p. 10; and W. Hoppe, *Erzbischof Wichmann von Magdeburg* [The Archbishop Wichmann of Magdeburg] (GSLM, Jahrgang 43-44 [1908-1909]), pp. 261ff.

Poppe, p. 32.

Świechowski, p. 265.

35 Askanas, *Sztuka płocka*, p. 53.

Chojnacki, *"Romańskie drzwi płockie—idea kopii...,"* p. 71.

Goldschmidt, *Die Bronzetüren von Novgorod und Gnesen*, p. 8.

Poppe, pp. 30 and 33.

Swarzenski, p. 78; Figures 466-467.

Walicki, *"Dekoracja architektury i jej wystrój artystyczny,"* p. 227; Pietrusińska and others, p. 744. The door is dated to the years between 1152 and 1156.

36 Askanas, *Brązowe drzwi płockie...*, pp. 24-27.

Askanas, *Sztuka płocka*, p. 53.

Dobrowolski, p. 105.

Gieysztor, *"Przed portalem płockiej katedry,"* pp. 9-10.

Goldschmidt, *Die Bronzetüren von Novgorod und Gnesen,* p. 8.

Lelewel, cited in Chojnacki, *"Romańskie drzwi płockie — idea kopii...,"* p. 71.

Poppe, pp. 32-33.

Walicki, *"Dekoracja architektury i jej wystrój artystyczny,* p. 227; Pietrusińska and others, p. 744.

37 Morelowski, *"Drzwi gnieźnieńskie, ich związki ze sztuką obcą...,"* p. 45.

Walicki, *"Dekoracja architektury i jej wystrój artystyczny,"* p. 227; Pietrusińska and others, p. 744.

38 Walicki, *"Dekoracja architektury i jej wystrój artystyczny,"* p. 227.

Zarnecki, *Romanesque Art,* p. 107.

39 Askanas, *Sztuka płocka,* p. 53.

40 Kessler, p. 181.

41 Kessler, p. 182.

42 Kessler, pp. 181-182. In addition, see Schapiro, *"On the Relation of Patron and Artist...,"* pp. 228-229.

43 Askanas, *Sztuka płocka,* p. 53.

Askanas, *Brązowe drzwi płockie...,* pp. 25, 27.

44 Munz, pp. 56-58.

45 Munz, p. 58.

46 Munz, p. 56. See also *Mistrza Wincentego kronika polska,* pp. 168, 170-172, 193. Frederick I Barbarossa's family connections led him to become involved both diplomatically and militarily in the dynastic struggle for succession among the rival sons of Polish King Bolesław III Krzywousty (The Wry Mouth), following his death in 1138. Frederick I attempted to safeguard the interests of Krzywousty's eldest son and eventual successor, Władysław II (1138-1146), Prince of Silesia and Cracow, and later the interest of Władysław's three sons (Bolesław *Wysoki,* 1127-1201; Mieszek Plątonogi,

✠

1131-1211; and Konrad, Bishop of Bamberg, circa 1139-circa 1202). Their mother, the wife of Władysław II, was Agnes, the stepsister of Conrad III, King of Germany (1138-1152), and the stepaunt of Frederick I Barbarossa.

47 Munz, p. 56.

"Wichmann of Magdeburg," *New Catholic Encyclopedia*, (New York: McGraw-Hill Book Company), Vol. 14 (1967), pp. 902-903.

48 Askanas, *Sztuka płocka*, p. 53.

Morelowski, *"Drzwi gnieźnieńskie, ich związki ze sztuką obcą...,"* pp. 45 and 94.

49 *Mistrza Wincentego kronika polska*, pp. 43 and 147.

50 Askanas, *Sztuka płocka*, pp. 50-52; Figures 540-542, 544-546.

Askanas, *Brązowe drzwi płockie...*, pp. 11-17; Figures 1-20, 23-24.

Gieysztor, *"Przed portalem płockiej katedry,"* p. 10.

Goldschmidt, *Die Bronzetüren von Novgorod und Gnesen*, pp. 7-26, 39-41; Plates II/1-II/70b.

Knapiński, pp. 26-27; Figures 27-29.

Leisinger, p. 3; Figures 1-7.

Rudziński, pp. 41-47.

Świechowski, pp. 67-68; Plates 189-198.

Walicki, *"Dekoracja architektury i jej wystrój artystyczny,"* Plates 1144-1164, 1167-1174; Pietrusińska and others, p. 744.

51 Świechowski, p. 67.

52 Rudziński, p. 44.

53 Świechowski, pp. 67-68.

54 Chojnacki, *"Drzwi płockie zawisły...,"* pp. 117, 120.

Chojnacki, *"O drzwiach płockich—streszczenie,"* p. 136.

55 Askanas, *Sztuka płocka*, p. 51.

Gieysztor, *"Przed portalem płockiej katedry,"* p. 10.

Knapiński, p. 27.

Morelowski, *"Drzwi gnieźnieńskie, ich związki ze sztuką obcą...,"* p. 94. He described the pictorial program on the door of the Cathedral of Płock as the interpretation of examples gathered from disparate sources.

Walicki, *"Dekoracja architektury i jej wystrój artystyczny,"* p. 228.

56 Askanas, *Sztuka płocka*, pp. 51-52.

Askanas, *Brązowe drzwi płockie...*, p. 12.

Gieysztor, *"Przed portalem płockiej katedry,"* p. 10.

Rudziński, pp. 42-46.

57 Kessler, pp. 175-176.

58 Kessler, p. 177.

59 Askanas, *Brązowe drzwi płockie...*, pp. 21 and 38.

Świechowski, p. 67.

60 Askanas, *Sztuka płocka*, p. 51.

61 Besides those actually discussed by some Polish sources as possible later replacements in the original Magdeburg-executed version? (The lower segments of the door's moldings, certain ornamental rivets, the image of the centaur, the portrait of the artist Avraam, and the tall, slender male figure of the so-called "Ruthenian dignitary" [the third row up from the bottom in the right wing].)

However, historians do not summarily agree. Poppe (p. 37) questions the later provenance of the slender figure, believing that it represents the original Magdeburg work. Gieysztor (*"Przed portalem płockiej katedry,"* p. 10) claims that Avraam's portrait is a Romanesque figure, while Świechowski (p. 265) believes it was made later. See also Askanas, *Sztuka płocka*, pp. 51 and 59, and *Brązowe drzwi płockie...*, pp. 12-13, 15-17; and Poppe, pp. 34-36.

The plate bearing the image of the centaur is a twentieth-century bas-relief, a replacement for a previous centaur plate, missing from the Novgorod door since 1947. The new cast was made from a copy of the Novgorod door executed in gypsum in 1886 and now in the collection of the Moscow Historical Museum. (See Chojnacki, *"Romańskie drzwi płockie—idea kopii...,"* p. 75; also Askanas, *Brązowe drzwi płockie...,* p. 17; and Poppe, pp. 34-35.) According to Poppe, the provenance of the original centaur plate still requires further study (p. 35). Some sources regard it as an authentic Romanesque work (Gieysztor, *"Przed portalem płockiej katedry,"* p. 9), while others argue that the relief was executed later in Novgorod (Askanas, *Brązowe drzwi płockie...,* p. 12 and 17; Świechowski, p. 265.

62 Poppe, p. 35.

CHAPTER FOUR

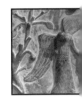

The Other Bronze Church Doors of the Era

While examining the extant Romanesque bronze church doors with regard to their iconographic content, decorative designs, and workmanship techniques, three principal groups are discernible:[1]

1. Eleventh-century doors whose workmanship and iconography point to bronze casters of Byzantium (Constantinople, now Istanbul), then the capital of the Eastern Roman Empire, where many bronze doors were commissioned for the churches on the Italian peninsula. (In the eleventh century the Byzantine Empire included the mid-southern portion of the Italian peninsula, known as the Duchy of Benevento.)[2]

2. Twelfth-century doors extant in present-day Italy and mainly credited to execution on Italian soil with native workmanship, although at times marked by Byzantine-art influences.

3. Doors credited to German workshops, dated to both the eleventh and the twelfth centuries.

The Romanesque-era bronze church doors range in size from the largest one, in the main entrance of the Cathedral of Monreale, Sicily (approximately 25 feet 6 inches high by 12 feet 1 inch wide), to the small door of the chapel-mausoleum at Canosa, in Italy's region of Apulia (5 feet 9 inches high).[3] In general, the doors consist of two wings constructed of wooden underbase with the surface covered by sheets of bronze—an alloy of copper, tin, zinc, and lead as well as occasional traces of other metals. Metallurgical analyses of the bronze alloy content in some of the doors (that were so tested) reveal a wide range of readings: about 66.5% to 92.25% copper and 0.12% to 16.32% tin; the remaining alloys were 0.87% to 20.1% lead and 0% to 17.9% zinc (Table IX).[4]

Placed across the middle register of the doors are the door knockers (door pulls), ranging from one pair to a series of eight, sculpted in bronze in the form of leonine masks that usually held rings in their jaws.

The bronze-sheeted surface of the doors is subdivided into decorative panel-shaped fields, forming a unified door-wing entity. The panels, filled with decorative imagery or script, are framed by the narrow moldings of bronze—flat and convex—usually enhanced by an ornamentation and placed at the outer edges of the panels, where they abut one another. The moldings, overlapping the edges of the panels, are subsequently riveted to the door's wooden core with nails (often bearing decorative heads) that secure the panels to their underbase.

In most of the church doors, bronze panels were cast individually.[5] Nonetheless, there exist a few examples of door wings in which the bronze sheeting of an entire wing was cast in one single piece (the doors in Hildesheim and Mainz, and also the left wing of the door leading to the chapel-tomb adjoining the Cathedral of Canosa), or a major portion may have been cast in one single piece, as it is suspected to be true for the left wing of the door at the Cathedral of Gniezno.[6]

In some of the Romanesque doors preponderant in the

✠

eleventh century and executed in Constantinople or in the Byzantine tradition of ornamentation, their principal or component figural imagery was incised into the bronze surface with fine grooves, and then the drawing was inlaid with a black metallic alloy consisting of copper, silver, lead, and sulfur. This is known as the niello technique. The details of the imagery were further enhanced by a colored (red and green) enamel, silver-leaf inlay, fine chasing (for instance, the doors at the cathedrals of Amalfi and Salerno, at the church in Atrani, and at Montecassino and Monte Sant'Angelo, as well as at St. Paul Outside-the-Walls in Rome or at the Basilica of St. Mark in Venice).

In the Byzantine mode of decoration, figural scenes were composed of stylized representations of hieratic personages from the Old and New Testaments, shown standing or seated singly and frontally underneath the arches. Also, for some of the eleventh-century bronze doors, their surface decoration may have consisted of cruciform emblems created in bronze and cast separately from the panels of the door to be riveted onto them (or, at times, rendered in the form of engravings on the panels); verbal texts incised either within panel-fields or on the surface of cruciform ornaments; motifs of engraved architectural forms (such as arches, for example); or designs of plant, arboreal, avian, or other animal derivation.

For other Romanesque bronze doors, and particularly those dated to the twelfth century, the pictorial figural decoration in their main panel-fields had undergone a change. Credited in a large measure to execution on Italian soil and to native Italian workmanship, even though at times showing Byzantine influences in the choice of ornament, their decoration was no longer defined by engraved, niello-inlaid, linear, hieratic figures or emblems, or script. Figural designs (and verbal passages) were often achieved by means of sculptured relief in bronze, in the so-called lost-wax (*cire perdue*)

✠

TABLE IX

Comparative Metallurgical Analyses of the Principal Alloys in the Metal Samples Examined in Some of the Bronze Doors of the Eleventh and Twelfth Centuries

Places	Date	Copper	Tin	Zinc	Lead
Augsburg, Cathedral of	1050-1065				
the right wing (plate 92)		66.5%	1%	0.7%	20.1%
border adjacent to the plate		69.6%	4%	0.4%	7.2%
Gniezno, Cathedral of	1170s to 1190s				
the right wing		86.82%	12.2%	0%	0.87%
the right ring holder		86.31%	9.47%	0%	4.08%
the left wing					
sample 1		90.12%	7.23%	tr.	2.51%
sample 2		91.98%	5.82%	tr.	1.92%
the left ring holder		92.25%	5.7%	0%	1.87%
Hildesheim, Cathedral of	1015				
the right wing		77.22%	8.5%	5.04%	8.64%
the left wing		76.56%	7.33%	4.3%	11.25%

	Date				
Mainz, Cathedral of	988-1009				
the right wing					
sample 1		80.11%	13.43%	(1.59%)	4.87%
sample 2		78.89%	14.34%	1.65%	(5.12%)
the left wing		74.18%	16.32%	2.27%	7.02%
Montecassino, Abbey of	1066				
the Maurus panels		81.59%	2.05%	10.65%	4.06%
St. Philip's panel (the reverse side)		82.50%	3.28%	11.23%	2.98%
Rome, Basilica of	1070				
St. Paul Outside-the-Walls		73.5%	0.12%	17.9%	8.48%
Venice, Basilica of	1112-1138 and ca. 1100				
St. Mark					
the Madonna door		78%	3%	9%	8%
St. Clement's Door		72.4%	2.2%	16.8%	8.6%
Verona, Basilica of	1085, 1138-1140, late 12th C.				
St. Zeno		90.17%	6.99%	0%	2.77%

process.[7] Characteristic of plasticity of forms—ranging from the low to the almost three-dimensional (for example, the doors of Benevento, Monreale, Pisa, Ravello, or Trani)—the figures assumed seemingly natural and mobile shapes and expressions that replaced the Byzantine tradition of linear abstraction and severity of the human figure.

Another group with a bas-relief decoration, dated to the eleventh- and twelfth-century ornamental bronze church doors, and credited in general to German workshops, is known from several examples in Europe. They include the doors in Augsburg, Mainz and Hildesheim, Germany; in Novgorod, Russia; and in Verona, Italy.

The three areas that—besides Byzantium and the Italian peninsula—had been enjoying a reputation for excelling in casting in bronze in eleventh- and twelfth-century Europe are known as the Lower Rhineland, the Meuse, and Saxony.[8]

--------- ✠ ---------

Byzantine-Style Bronze Doors
The Cathedral of Amalfi[9]
(Figures 14-16)

The cathedral's door (dated to 1060 or toward the year 1065) is constructed of twenty-four panels, twelve of them forming a wing. Twenty panels are adorned with large, single bronze cruciforms growing from their base of a stylized foliage, symbols of the Tree of Life, or the *arbor vitae* (the tree whose fruit, if eaten by man, was to give him immortality [Genesis 3:22]). An incised text appears on, or below, some of the cruciforms (the second row of panels from the bottom of the door). The door's four central panels contain traces of nielloed engravings with red and green enamel and silver leaf. The inscriptions in Greek and Latin indicate that these images originally represented the figures of Christ, the

Virgin Mary, St. Peter, and St. Andrew, the latter two as the patrons of the cathedral and of the door.

Three pairs of leonine-head ring holders are arranged across the middle register of the door.

One of the cruciforms (now lost) bore an inscription in Greek, crediting the execution of the door to Simeone (di Siria?) and to Sta (urachios [Staurakios]?), perhaps of Greek or Syrian origin. The door was a gift of Pantaleone, the elder son of Mauro, members of a rich and politically influential Amalfi merchant family of Mauroni whose three generations bearing the names of Mauro or Pantaleone had been known as donors of the bronze doors for the churches on the Italian peninsula: at Amalfi, Montecassino, the Sanctuary of Monte Sant'Angelo, and St. Paul Outside-the-Walls in Rome. The doors were executed in Constantinople, where the family had maintained a residence, and had large commercial interests.

The Church of San Salvatore del Bireto at Atrani[10] (Figure 17)

According to the dedicatory inscription, the door was executed in 1087. Cast in Constantinople, the door was commissioned by Pantaleone, the son of Pantaleone Viarecta, perhaps of the Atrani family, distinct from the Amalfi family of Mauroni. The door consists of twenty-four decorative panel-fields. Like the Amalfi and the Salerno doors, it is principally decorated with applied foliated cruciforms in bronze. Only four central panel-fields are filled with engraved and nielloed images of frontally standing under the arches, single figures of Christ, the Virgin Mary, St. Sebastian, and St. Pantaleone.

The Abbey of Montecassino[11]
(Figures 18-19)

The bronze door in the abbey's main portal was originally commissioned in Constantinople in 1066 by the abbey's Abbot Desiderius, as a gift from Mauro (Maurus), the father of Pantaleone, the donor of the bronze door at the Cathedral of Amalfi. The subsequent tragic events of the earthquake in 1349, and the bombardment of the abbey during World War II, had changed the components of the door. The present form of the door (measuring about 10 feet 11 inches by 5 feet 7 inches), restored after its panels—twisted and deformed by the fire—have been salvaged from the war ruins, consist of forty fields. The main thirty-six panels are mostly filled with engraved and nielloed inscriptions in Latin, enumerating the abbey's church dependencies. A predella at the base of the door comprises two large panels (each consisting of three plates) bearing four applied bronze cruciforms flanking the dedicatory texts, crediting the door to Maurus of Amalfi. The plate on the right also includes the date of 1066, as the door's origin. Beneath the predella, there are two lateral-shaped panels devoid of any decorative contents.

It has been a matter of dispute to what extent the current door represents a surviving decoration of the door's original eleventh-century ornamental program. It is suggested that only the predella panels with the dedicatory texts and the crosses date from the original 1066 door. Also, the remains of the ornamentation existing on the reverse sides of the nine of the door's current panel-fields suggest that they might be a surviving decoration of the original door, executed, perhaps, by Staurachios, and rendered in nielloed engravings of the Apostles, and patriarchs from the Old Testament, presented as the single, frontally standing figures.

S. Michele Sul Gargano, Monte Sant'Angelo[12]
(Figures 20-23)

According to a legend, the Bishop of Siponto, Lorenzo Maiorano, experienced miraculous visions in which St. Michael the Archangel had appeared to him in a grotto at the Monte Gargano, near the Adriatic coast in Italy. Following the archangel's expressed wish, a sanctuarium consecrated to him and other angels was erected on that site. The edifice's bronze door has twenty-four rectangular panels filled with images and inscriptions in Latin. The images, rendered in silver-inlaid engravings, heightened with red- and green-colored enamel outlines and inlays of silver leaf, depict a random collection of episodes in which appearances of St. Michael the Archangel (the Angel of the Lord) are described in the Old and New Testaments. They also record the archangel's appearances before the Bishop of Siponto, the archangel's crowning of two early Roman Christian martyrs, the husband and wife Sts. Cecilia and Valerian, and the appearance of two angels before St. Martin of Tours. One of the panels on the door's right wing is filled with the inscribed text of a dedicatory prayer stating that the door originated in 1076 in Constantinople, thanks to DMNO Pantaleone, but the door's maker remains unknown.

A sequence of six leonine-head door pulls, arranged in pairs, is placed across the middle register of the sanctuarium's door.

The Cathedral of Salerno[13]
(Figure 24)

The decoration of the cathedral's bronze door is a variant on the decorative schema of the Amalfi and Atrani doors. Composed of fifty-four small panel-fields, twenty-seven in each wing, the door is embellished with applied, single bronze cruciform ornaments. Only the eight panels in the middle zone of the door are filled with the engraved, sil-ver-inlaid contents. A horizontal row of six panels bears fig-ures identified by the inscriptions in Greek. They are frontal-ly posed, standing renditions of the Virgin Mary, Sts. Matthew, Peter, Paul, Simon and Christ. Above these saintly images, there are two panels filled with different contents. The panel on the left wing bears the engraved image of a Fountain of Life, flanked by two griffins and a pair of eagles; according to the text filling the panel on the right wing, the door, dedicated to St. Matthew, the door's patron saint, was a gift of a Salerno Prince, Landolfo Butrumile, and of his wife, Guisana Sebaston. Their figures, identified in script, are rendered on either side of the image of St. Matthew.

Four tiny leonine heads are sculpted on the panel mold-ing across the middle register of the door.

This work of art, dating to the years between 1087 and 1099, is regarded as perhaps executed in Constantinople.

The Basilica of San Marco in Venice[14, 15]
Two doors. (Figures 25-26)

A trio of doors inside the vestibule of the basilica's western façade, leading into the interior of the church, includes the two doors that occupy a distinguished place among the remains of Byzantine-style art in the West, linking them strongly to the southern Italian bronze doors. The basilica's central door is called the Madonna Door,[14] and the door on the right is named after St. Clement.[15] The dates of the exe-cution of either of the doors, and their provenance, have not been documented and remain rather speculative. The doors' origin is estimated to either "sometime" in the "second decade" of the twelfth century, or between 1112 and 1138 (the central door) and around 1100, or the eighties of the eleventh century (the right-side door). Other evaluations, disputing that dating, have variously assigned the doors to the thirteenth, fourteenth, or even sixteenth centuries.

The principal decoration of the panel-fields in both of the doors is formed of the engraved figural images, inlaid with silver and accented with fine chasing. However, the Madonna Door's images, thought to be the product of a possible cooperation between the Venetian and Byzantine artists, show a different technique in which, in addition to the silver inlay, a colored enamel was also introduced. The Madonna Door's images, identified by the inscriptions in Latin, depict the figures of King David, the Virgin Mary, Christ, St. John the Baptist, the Archangels Michael and Gabriel, the twelve Apostles, saints, and the Old Testament prophets bearing the scrolls with biblical quotations in the Greek language.

The Madonna's Door's forty-eight panels (twenty-four in each wing), arranged in the eight three-panel horizontal rows, include bronze cruciform ornaments (the top row) and a stylized floral decoration in the form of four large lozenge-shaped petals with rosette centers (the lowest of the rows). A sequence of four pairs of door pulls in the form of small leonine masks, holding rings in their jaws, is placed across the middle register of the door.

On the door's panel depicting the figure of St. Mark, the patron saint of Venice, a man's silhouette is represented kneeling at St. Mark's feet. The inscription above him declares: *"Leo da Molino hoc ōp fieri iussit,"* pointing to the likelihood that the work was commissioned by Leo da Molino, a rich merchant who, according to historical sources, served as a financial administrator or the "Procurator" of the Basilica of San Marco in 1112. (He lived until the year 1138).

The second door at the basilica, the so-called *Porta di San Clemente*, comprises twenty-eight decorative panel-fields, fourteen in each wing, with two panels to a row, larger in size than those in the Madonna Door. The central area of the San Clemente Door has an assemblage of religious images, showing Christ, the Virgin Mary, and the twelve Apostles, joined by saints. The personages, crowned with nimbi, are shown singly, standing frontally beneath the rounded arches, formed of undulating, lobed renditions of a stylized vegetal stem. These figures of both the Latin and the Orthodox rites, adorning twenty-two out of twenty-eight panels of the door, are identified by the engraved inscriptions in Greek. In the top row of the door, two of the panels contain the motif of an engraved cross (with three horizontal bars) placed underneath an arch; while the four panels in the lowest row of the door are filled with the engravings of abstract forms of animals, birds, and vegetal stems, and palmettes. Six small leonine heads, arranged in pairs, decorate the middle register of the door.

The Basilica of St. Paul Outside-the-Walls in Rome[16] (Figures 27-28)

The door that once had hung in the basilica's main entrance is now on view in the basilica's museum. The monument had been damaged by fire in 1823, and its restoration did not take place until the 1960s. The door's original appearance will never be known, for during the restoration from fragments saved from the conflagration, the door's fifty-four panels were apparently haphazardly reassembled, without any thematic order. The engraved and nielloed images are identified in Greek and Syriac. The images in the upper panels of the left wing depict episodes from the lives of the Virgin Mary and Christ, starting with scenes of the Annunciation and ending with the Pentecost. Other images show standing figures of the Apostles, or their martyrdom, scenes of death and burial. There are also images of the Old

Testament prophets who stand singly beneath the round arches. Two of the side panel-fields in the middle zone of the door contain ornamental crosses; two panels at the bottom of the door are decorated with stylized eagles; and two central panels bear the inscriptions in Latin dedicating the door to St. Paul, and stating that the door was a gift of Malfigeno Pantaleone.

A kneeling figure shown between the representations of Christ and of St. Paul, the patron of the basilica, has been interpreted as that of the door's donor. An inscription (which perished in fire) stated in Greek and Syriac that the door was cast by Simeone and Staurachio Tuchitos of Scio. A Greek sign uncovered during the door's restorations also revealed the name of Teodoro as the door's artist designer. The two-wing door, commissioned in Constantinople in 1070, measures 16 feet 6 inches by 11 feet 3 inches.

Twelfth-Century Italian Bronze Doors Sculpted Totally, or in Part, in Bas-Relief, Incorporating at Times Some Byzantine-Style Elements The Cathedral of Benevento[17] (Figures 29-30)

The bronze door that once adorned the main entrance of the cathedral exists at present only in fragments, salvaged from the ruins of World War II and preserved in the *biblioteca capitolare* of Benevento. The door's origin (by an unknown artist) is ascribed to either the second half of the twelfth century or to its end. It has been said that its decoration, "modified" by certain Byzantine-style elements, expresses the "Italian love of vivacious narrative."

A prewar photograph shows the door composed of seventy-two ornamental panels, thirty-six in each wing. The door's imagery is rendered in high bas-relief of roughly molded projections and depressions, achieving a three-dimensional quality in the rendition of heads and gesticulating hands and in four door pulls in the form of leonine and griffin heads holding rings in their jaws.

An interesting difference is observed in the treatment of figural representations and architectural structures depicted on the door's panels. In the upper panels, rounded arches provide the background for mobile, naturalistic group scenes from the life of Christ and the Virgin Mary. In the four bottom rows of panels, the motif of a pointed arch encloses twenty-four figures of the ecclesiastic hierarchy. In addition to the Archbishop of Benevento, the figures show the assemblage of suffragan bishops of Benevento. The latter stand immobile, single, frontally-posed, holding the crosiers, and raising the right hands in the act of blessing. Each figure is identified by an inscription.

Canosa di Puglia[18]
(Figures 31-32)

The chapel-mausoleum (adjoining the Cathedral of Canosa) has a small bronze door (about 5 feet 9 inches high) that was executed shortly after the year 1111, commemorating Bohemund (Boemondo) I, prince of Antioch and a hero of the Crusades (1065-1111).

Some art historians regard this door (imitating the Byzantine style) as "probably made in Italy." But other sources say that it is the first one cast in bronze in Italy by an Italian craftsman (perhaps Rogerius of Melfie [Amalfi?] Campanarum [the meaning of the word "Campanarum" is controversial], whose name is incised on the left wing).

The door's wings are of unequal size; the right one is smaller than the left one. The left wing was cast in one piece; the right wing might have been cast in three or, perhaps, four parts and subsequently joined (but without the usual support of a base of wood, which is absent in the Canosa door).

✠

The ornamentation of the door is achieved by means of sculpturing in bronze combined with the niello-inlaid engravings. Rendered in bas-relief are two large disks centrally placed on the right wing's panels and filled densely with an overall Muslim arabesque of vegetal and zoomorphic content; and on the left wing there are three large rosettes, rimmed in the sculpted geometric pattern of a "Saracenic character" and embellished in their centers by either incised lettering, a sculpted demonic-looking leonine mask, or a stylized, multipetaled flower.

The niello-inlaid engravings depict figures clad in toga-like garments and long outer cloaks in the two central zones of the right wing; and on the left wing incised inscriptions in Latin, extolling the deeds of Bohemund, fill the areas unoccupied by the rosettes.

A pair of nonmatching doorknobs is sculpted in the form of lion-head and humanoid masks. In addition, six half-masks possessing human features are placed along the borders of the right wing.

The Baptistery of St. John Lateran in Rome[19]
(Figure 33)

The dating of a bronze door in one of the baptistery's chapels dedicated to St. John the Evangelist remains largely speculative.

Although some art research sources claim that it was the work of the early Christian period—originated, perhaps, in the fifth century—the sources of the seventeenth century (Joannis Ciampini Romani) and the nineteenth century (Georges Rohault de Fleury) disagree. On the basis of the Latin inscriptions engraved on the right wing (upper field) and the left wing (the archivault of the image of arcades), they contend, the door's execution took place in 1195, during the fifth year of the pontificate of Pope Celestine III

(1191-1198). The door is said to have been commissioned by a papal chamberlain, the Cardinal Cencio. Two artist-brothers, Ubertino and Pietro, originally of Lausanne or Piacenza, but schooled in Rome, are recorded as the door's casting masters.

The door's two wings are divided into four decorative fields embellished in silver-inlaid engravings and bas-relief.

The engraved decoration records architectural elements (the left wing) of two arcades, flanked by two bell towers (believed to depict towers of the Lateran Basilica); and, in the right wing, the battlements and towers (possibly showing the old Lateran Palace, the seat of the popes, adjoining the basilica, for which this door was originally executed).

The motifs rendered in bas-relief represent a bearded man clothed in ecclesiastical vestments (chasuble and cowl) and holding an orblike globular object and book (it is believed to represent the Pope Celestine III); and a figure of a crowned woman standing under one of the arcades (possibly a symbol of the Church).

The Cathedral of Monreale
(Duomo Santa Maria La Nuova)[20, 21]
Two doors. (Figures 34-35)

The cathedral's two bronze doors (in the main, western entrance, and in the northern wall) were both executed in the twelfth century—five years apart—by different artists.

The inscription in Latin on the right wing of the main door states that it was executed in 1186[20] by Bonannus, a citizen of Pisa. It is the largest of the Romanesque bronze church doors known, measuring 25 feet 6 inches by 12 feet 1 inch. The door's top is unusually shaped into an ogive curve, corresponding with the ogive arch of the entrance's stone portico that encloses the bronze door. The door's surface comprises forty-six decorative panel-fields, twenty-three in each wing. Those situated in the central zone of the door depict episodes from the New and Old Testaments, identified by Latin inscriptions rendered in bas-relief. In the door's two top panel-fields (of a double width) are representations of the Virgin Mary enthroned between four cherubim (the left wing), and of Christ in glory, surrounded by the angels and cherubim (the right wing). The door's lowest four panel-fields (larger in size than the door's central area panels) contain renditions of paired lions and griffins.

The door's imagery is elegantly sculptured in medium relief that emerges from the surrounding flat bronze background in flowing outlines and planes of the forms.

The Cathedral of Monreale's side door (1190)[21] bears the sign proclaiming *"Barisanus Tranensis me fecit,"* the creator of the main doors for the cathedrals of Ravello and Trani.

This door is smaller in size (about 13 feet 9 inches high by 7 feet wide) than the main door of the cathedral. The twenty-eight panel-fields, sculpted in a softly modeled low- and medium-high relief, are crowned by images of Christ in glory placed in the two central panels of the highest row of panel-fields. The images of Christ are situated between the images of St. John the Baptist and of the Prophet Elias. The remaining panels are filled in the largest part with figures of the Apostles and saints presented singly, seated frontally under rounded arches. The pictures showing St. George and St. Eustathius are flanking a pair of leonine heads emerging from their background bronze wall decorated with avian and dragon motifs.

The four plates in the lowest row of the door containing escutcheons and a figure of youth (described by some sources as depicting Bacchus) are regarded to be a later replacement in the door's decoration.

All of the door's images are presented in individual square- or arch-shaped frames, richly ornamented with stylized vegetal motifs. The inscriptions in Latin identifying a few of the figural images are incised into the bronze surface.

The Cathedral of Pisa[22]
(Figure 36)

The *Porta di San Ranieri* in the cathedral's main entrance was executed (according to extant chronicles) about 1180-1186 by Bonannus *civis Pisanus*, the creator of the main door of the Cathedral of Monreale. His assistant is said to have been named Wilhelmus.

The door (15 feet 4 inches high by 9 feet 8 inches wide) was cast in twenty-four panels. The door's twenty central panel-fields (almost square shaped) show scenes from the New Testament, starting with the Annunciation and Visitation and concluding with the Ascension of Our Lord and Pentecost. (The content of images is developed from the bottom of the door upward and read horizontally across the area of both wings from the left to the right.)

The two uppermost panels of the door and the two panels at the bottom are larger than the central panels and are rectangular. The uppermost panels contain the images of Christ in glory (the left wing) and the Madonna enthroned (the right wing). Both representations are flanked by angels.

The two bottom panels contain images of the Old Testament's prophets. These figures, holding unfurled scrolls, are depicted seemingly in motion while conversing with one another under the row of twelve palm trees.

Almost all of the images are identified by the Latin text rendered in bas-relief. The door's imagery is elegantly presented in softly modeled, clearly contoured relief, ranging from a low to a high sculpturing.

The Cathedral of Ravello (Duomo San Pantaleone)[23]
(Figure 37)

The bronze door (12 feet 5 inches high by 8 feet 9 inches wide) in the cathedral's main entrance was executed by the "Great Apulian brass-founder" Barisanus of Trani, the creator also of the side door of the Cathedral of Monreale and the main door in the Cathedral of Trani. His work is described as showing a close relationship to the Byzantine tradition of art in bronze.

The Ravello door is composed of fifty-four small, rectangular panels, decorated in the bas-relief imagery except for a panel bearing an engraved, silver-inlaid text in Latin identifying the year 1179 as the time of the door's execution. The panel also holds the name of Sergio Muscetola (Musetule), a patrician of Ravello who, with his wife and family, offered the door to the cathedral to honor the Virgin Mary.

The bas-relief imagery presents duplicate versions (the top row panels of the wings) of representations of Christ in glory surrounded by the symbols of the four Evangelists. These two central panels are flanked by the panels depicting genuflecting angels. The remaining panel-fields of the door show a mélange of images, often depicting duplicate versions of scenes; among them, Christ's deposition from the Cross and his descent into hell, the Madonna and Child, Sts. George and Eustathius, men with bows and arrows, and gladiators. Other images show the Apostles and various religious personages posed seated. A pair of lion-head door pulls (only one has a ring in its jaws) is ornamented with pairs of birds and dragons. Most of the images are identified by engraved Latin insciptions. The door's two lowest rows of panel-fields contain a series of twelve symbols of the Tree of Life, guarded by lions and dragons.

The area of figural panels of the door is contrasted by a wide filigree-filled frame that encloses the top and the two vertical sides of the Ravello door.

The Cathedral of Trani (San Nicola Pellegrino)[24]
(Figures 38-40)

The cathedral is notable for its bronze door in the main portal executed in 1175 by Barisanus of Trani (*Barisanus Tranensis*), an Italian artist who also created the Cathedral of Ravello's main door and the side door of the Cathedral of Monreale. His name is engraved on one of the Trani door panels that shows St. Nicholas the Pilgrim, the patron of the city of Trani. It has been assumed that a kneeling figure shown at the feet of St. Nicholas in all probability symbolizes the figure of the artist Barisanus. The door (15 feet 9 inches high by 8 feet 9 inches wide) is subdivided into thirty-two image-ornamented panel-fields, surrounded by a wide archlike border of rectangular plates filled with filigree ornamentation. The arch's shape corresponds with the arch of the stone portico of the door's entrance. The door's imagery depicts in bas-relief the multiple subjects. The images of Christ in majesty shown between the adoring angels crown the uppermost row of the panels. Below, scenes of Our Lord's deposition from the Cross and his descent into hell are combined with the pictures of the Madonna and Child, the Apostles, the Prophet Elias, Sts. George and Eustathius, gladiators, archers, and depictions of a Biblical theme of the Tree of Life, centered between the pairs of lions and winged dragons. In the panel-fields, accommodating two door pulls in the form of leonine heads with rings in their jaws, the forms of birds and dragons are serving as the background.

In the ornamental schema of the doors in Trani and Monreale, their artist applied a common motif of embellishing each image individually by enclosing it within a richly ornamented frame made of a pattern of stylized stem-and-palmette design.

The Cathedral of Troia [25, 26]
Two doors. (Figures 41-44)

This cathedral on the Apulian plain of Italy possesses two bronze doors, commissioned by the Bishop Willelmus (Guglielmo) II. The main portal's door was executed in 1119;[25] the side door was made in 1127.[26] The execution of both doors is usually attributed to the Italian artist Oderisius of Benevento. However, this opinion has been disputed for the reference to Oderisius as the creator of the work appears exclusively on the side door.

The doors' surface decoration, described as bearing notable influences of Byzantine and Norman art, is rendered in silver-inlaid engravings and sculpted bronze ranging from low to high relief, with some of the ornamentation nearly three-dimensional.

In the main door there are twenty-eight almost square panel-fields, fourteen in each wing, arranged in seven horizontal rows two panel-fields wide. Each row differs from the others in the content of its decoration. (1) The first and uppermost row contains the engraved and nielloed figures, identified in script as Oderisius, Berardus, Christ, Willelmus, and the Apostles St. Peter and St. Paul. (2) The following row is filled with four heads of lionlike monsters sculpted in bronze with rings in their jaws. (3) The third row displays armorial emblems (accompanied with inscriptions) executed in low relief; they actually represent a sixteenth- to seventeenth-century replacement decoration of the door. (4) In the central row of the door, two bas-relief emblems in the shape of the Cross arc flanking the door's two door pulls in the form of winged, serpentine, dog-headed dragons; their three-dimensional bodies sculpted in bronze detach themselves from the wall of the door. (5) Another row shows four lion heads sculpted in bronze. (6) Four saintly figures stand on individual pedestals—rendered in engravings. (7) The lowest of the rows bears the engraved dedicatory inscriptions that include the date of the door's creation, and the names of the Bishop of Troia, Willelmus II, and the Pope Calixtus II.

Small masks resting on a motif of a four-petal floral ornament are distributed at the intersections of the panel-moldings crisscrossing throughout the door.

The exterior of the second, or side, door (1127) of the Cathedral of Troia consists of the twenty-four rectangular panels, twelve in each wing. The door is divided into two uneven areas (twelve panels [above] and eight panels [below]) by the middle-zone row of panels, adorned with four bronze door pulls sculpted in the shape of big, monstrous lion heads with rings in their jaws. The remaining panels are ornamented in the Byzantine-style technique of the silver-inlaid engravings, representing figural images and inscriptions. These include the representations of the eight bishops of Troia, the predecessors of the Bishop Willelmus II, the donor of the Troia cathedral's doors, as well as the text of his dedicatory pronouncement.

On the door's panel molding situated immediately below the panels with the lion heads, the engraved inscription states that the door's maker was Oderisius of Benevento.

Eleventh- and Twelfth-Century Bronze Doors Mainly Credited to German Workshops The Cathedral of Augsburg[27] (Figure 45)

Although in all probability this bronze door was created on German soil (by an unknown maker), it has been described as "stylistically...related to the Italo-Byzantine tradition of doors manufactured in Constantinople for Italian churches and to those subsequently manufactured in Italy after Byzantine models."

The door, hanging in the cathedral's southern wall, is dated between 1050-1060, or probably to 1065. In contrast to the doors in two other German cathedrals in Hildesheim and Mainz, the Augsburg door was cast in thirty-five separate panels. The wings of the door are characteristically asymmetrical. Though of the same height (approximately 13 feet 1 inch), they possess an unequal width. The right wing (about 3 feet 3 inches) contains fourteen rectangular plates arranged in two vertical rows of seven plates each. The left wing (4 feet 2 inches wide) has three vertical rows of twenty-one plates, the middle row consisting of much narrower rectangular plates than those forming the two adjacent rows of the wing.

The decorative images on the plates are sculpted in low relief, softly modeled and outlined; their content is assembled without regard for coherence of themes. Some of the images appear to replicate the same subject more than once. The decorative program includes scenes from the life of Samson and scenes relating to Genesis; other images portray single centaurs, lions, a bear, a crowned warrior king, a man with a shield, a man standing under a tree, a man eating grapes and a woman feeding a flock of birds, a tree with two serpents writhing under it, men accompanied by serpents, and other male figures that are not identifiable. The door's two ring holders are in the form of demonic masks, combining both human and leonine features. The eighteen tiny humanoid and animal masks, sculpted in bronze, are each characterized by their own individual facial features and expressions and placed at the intersections of the plain bronze moldings, crisscrossing the wings' surface vertically and horizontally.

The Cathedral of Hildesheim[28]
(Figures 46-47)

The bronze door situated in the western façade of the cathedral was originally intended for the nearby Abbey Church of St. Michael and was subsequently transferred to the cathedral. The name of the door's donor Bernward (*Bernwardus Episcopus*) and the date of the door's execution (MXV) are inscribed along the middle register of both wings.

The door's wings were each cast as "solid entities" in one piece. The door is 15 feet 5 inches high by 7 feet 5 inches wide. Each of the wings is subdivided into eight large, rectangular, horizontal panel-fields. Their decorative imagery is executed in relief of "generous modeling and swelling volumes," varying from a shallow bas-relief to the three-dimensional projections emerging from the flat bronze wall of the door panels (particularly in the area of the heads).

The left wing's imagery—reading from the top downward—depicts scenes of the creation of man and of his fall, Adam's subsequent labors and Eve nursing her child, as well as scenes of conflict between Abel and Cain. The right wing—starting at the bottom and reading upward—addresses itself to various episodes from the life of Christ, his passion and the Resurrection, after a beginning scene of the Annunciation and ending with a *"Noli me tangere"* scene between Christ and Mary Magdalen.

Two leonine-head door pulls accentuate the wings of the door.

The Cathedral of Mainz[29]
(Figure 48)

The bronze door (12 feet 1 inch high by 6 feet 6 inches wide) dates to "before 1011," or to the time more closely defined as between 988 and 1009. It was executed by the order of the Archbishop of Mainz, Willigisus (Willigis), 975-1011, as recorded in a Latin inscription. The inscription also bears the artist's name Berengerus (Beringer?) (*huius operis artifex*), on the horizontal upper, middle and low borders of the door. The door's wings, each cast in one piece, have a simply decorated surface comprising four large, rectangular, vertically placed panel-fields.

The two upper fields are filled with Latin script. The two lower ones have plain grounds; each contains a single leonine head, sculpted in high relief, holding a ring in its open-fanged muzzle. (However, these ring holders have been described as later additions to the door, dated variously to the twelfth or thirteenth centuries.)

The Basilica of San Zeno Maggiore[30]
(Figures 49-50)

The Verona basilica's bronze door (said to be approximately 16 feet 4 inches high, with its left wing 6 feet 4 inches wide and the right wing's width measuring 6 feet 1 3/5 inches) hangs in the edifice's western façade. The door consists of forty-eight square-shaped panels, cast individually. Twenty-four panels, arranged in eight rows of a three-panel width, make up each wing.

The present form of the door's decoration does not allow for assuming the same execution date for both wings. Most of the panels in the left wing, earlier stylistically, are usually dated to the late eleventh century, with others credited to the years 1138-1140 or, as some sources suggest, to near 1100 (1085) or to the years between 899-1117. The rest of the images reflecting the art of a later dating, are held to date to the late twelfth century (or its second half).

The door was perhaps executed in Germany and then transported to Verona. It has been credited mainly to Saxonian artists of the Magdeburg workshop. Nonetheless, some of the reliefs in the right wing are considered the possible work of an Italian artist. It is surmised that there must have been at least three artistic hands involved. (The names of Niccolò, Willelmus, and Stefano Lagerinus have been suggested by some art historians.)

The door's imagery is rendered in bas-relief densely filling the space of the panels. But certain elements, such as the heads, upper torsos, and lower and upper limbs, thrust aggressively outward from the panel background in a three-dimensional plasticity of high relief. The forms, once described as *"souvent barbare, presque sauvage"* [often barbaric, almost brutal], are sharply delineated with rigid contours and simplified body shapes, and their mass is accented with the variety of engraved strong linear patterns and dots.

The imagery on the door in Verona relates to both the New and Old Testaments. It begins in the upper part of the left wing with scenes of the Annunciation, the Nativity, and the Flight into Egypt, and continues depicting scenes from the life of Christ, Our Lord's Passion and the Crucifixion, ending with the images of the women at the sepulcher, and Christ's descent into hell. However, the succeeding panels represent a variety of themes assembled in a haphazard manner. Some of them relate to the life of St. John the Baptist, including his beheading, Salome's dance and Herod's banquet. Other scenes are depictions of Adam and Eve, their expulsion from Paradise, and their labors after the Fall.

The theme of Adam and Eve is being continued onto the right wing with the creation of Eve, the temptation, and the

✠

condemnation of Adam and Eve, followed by a repeated scene of their expulsion from Paradise. Succeeding scenes continue to picture various events of the Old Testament. Among them: a fratricidal conflict between Cain and Abel, Noah's ark, Noah's curse of Ham, his son, God appears to Abraham, the sacrifice of Isaac, Abraham's expulsion of Hagar, Aaron's staff transformed into a serpent, the Prophet Balaam riding the ass, the tree of Jesse, Nebuchadnezzar, King of Babylon, the sacrifice of Isaac and Noah's ark (a repetition of the themes shown earlier), and St. Michael overcoming a dragon.

The panel-fields also accommodate the two nonmatching door pulls (with the now missing rings), representing a bearded male head wearing a helmetlike covering, and a mask of a lionlike creature.

Two other panels are devoted to scenes from the life of St. Zeno (the patron of the basilica): They show the legates of the Emperor Gallen (Galienus) pleading with the saint to heal the Emperor's ill daughter, and, after the daughter was cured, depicting the bareheaded Emperor offering in gratitude his imperial crown to St. Zeno.

In addition, the Verona door's figural imagery sculpted in bronze includes (1) a series of human and leonine masks placed at the intersections of the panel moldings subdividing the surface of the door, and (2) an incomplete row of small figures along the vertical closing edge of the door's right wing.

They depict figures standing singly beneath the rounded arches: Among them, one discerns ecclesiastic personages; a rendition of Samson, personifying physical strength; and a man at work, holding a hammer in his hand.

✠

NOTES: CHAPTER FOUR

1 Diehl, p. 237.

Zarnecki, *Romanesque Art*, pp. 120 and 125.

2 Zarnecki, *Romanesque Art*, pp. 120 and 157.

Zarnecki, *Art of the Medieval World*, p. 261 (the work is Islamic-inspired); p. 256 (Western and Byzantine art met in Italy; Apulia and Calabria remained part of the Byzantine Empire for many centuries).

Louis L. Snyder, *A Survey of European Civilization* (Harrisburg: The Telegraph Press, 1945), Vol. 1, pp. 180-197.

3 Knapiński, pp. 21 and 24.

Zarnecki, *Romanesque Art*, p. 125.

4 von Boeckler, *Die Bronzetür von San Zeno*, p. 40.

Goldschmidt, *Die Deutschen Bronzetüren des Frühen Mittelalters*, pp. 13 and 15.

Laging, p. 131.

Matthiae, p. 20.

Dziekoński and Wesołowski, pp. 124-129, 136-139, 141-142, 156-161.

5 Dziekoński and Wesołowski, p. 139.

Kleinbauer, p. 280.

Laging, p. 130.

6 Dziekoński and Wesołowski, pp. 137, 139, 155.

Kleinbauer, p. 281.

Künstler, p. 172.

Laging, p. 130.

Morelowski, "*Drzwi gnieźnieńskie, ich związki ze sztuką obcą a problem rodzimości,*" p. 45.

7 The first adequate technical description of that method, traditionally practiced in executing decorative brass objects for ecclesiastical purposes, was described around 1200 by

Theophilus (known also as Rugerus), a Westphalian (or perhaps Rhenish) monk and priest, in the *De Diversis Artibus: Seu Diversarum Artium Schedula, Libri III* [About Various Arts, Three Volumes], translated with notes by Robert Hendrie (London: John Murray, Albemarle Street, 1847), pp. 311, 313, 319, 321, 325, 337, 353, 357, 359, 363, 365, 367, 437. See also Georgius Agricola, *De Re Metallica* [About the Objects in Metal], translated from the first Latin edition of 1556 by Herbert Clark Hoover and Lou Henry Hoover (New York: Dover Publications, 1950), pp. 312, 405, 410, 461, 609. In addition, a description of the lost-wax method may be found in Dziekoński and Wesołowski, pp. 139-140, 142-153.

According to Theophilus, that method called for (1) executing the original model in wax; (2) building a mold made of clay, the stage during which a sculpted decoration on the wax model was projected under pressure onto the surface of wet clay; (3) melting off the original wax model; and (4) replacing it in the mold by flowing molten metal (an alloy whose principal components were ores of copper, tin, and zinc, or calamine); (5) opening the mold and finishing and refining the surface of the cast object.

Theophilus detailed many aspects of the casting procedure, such as, for example, a preparation of the clay mixture; the soundness, dryness, and evenness of the mold surface; the application of varied degrees of heat intensity; as well as the cooling process or the escapement of gases during the pouring of metal into the mold.

He also discussed the steps that were to be taken in the preparation of the workplace, furnace, and crucibles, and listed the required tools, such as anvils, hammers, pincers, files, and sculpting, scraping, or cutting instruments, along with the instruments for malleable work. He also cautioned (see Hendrie, p. 363) that casting work requires not "slothful, but agile and diligent workmen, lest through neglect of any kind either the mold be broken, or one may hinder or hurt the other, or provoke him to anger, which is above all to be guarded against."

It was easier to execute a bronze surface of the door in separate small castings and then join the parts rather than engage in the complexity of large castings. The number and the division of cast parts of a wing of the door, as well as the traces of joins (or metallurgical bonds) at the edges of sections in the bronze sheeting of the door's surface, render the data from which it is possible to deduce the manner of a casting process applied in the execution of individual doors. (See Dziekoński and Wesołowski, pp. 150-151).

8 Zarnecki, *Romanesque Art*, p. 118.

9 Bertaux, Vol. 1, part 2, pp. 51, 403-405, 408-409.

Herbert Bloch, *Monte Cassino in the Middle Ages* (Cambridge, Massachusetts: Harvard University Press, 1986, three volumes), Vol. 1, part 2, pp. 140-141, 156, 160; Vol. 3, Figures 58-63.

Dalton, pp. 618-619.

Diehl, p. 237.

Focillon, p. 46.

Kleinbauer, pp. 279-281.

Kalinowski, *"O nowo odkrytych inskrypcjach na drzwiach gnieźnieńskich,"* p. 398.

Knapiński, p. 19.

Laging, p. 130.

Leisinger, p. 8; Plates 147-148.

Cardinal Ildefonso Schuster, *La Basilica e il Monastero di S. Paolo fuori le Mura* [The Basilica and the Monastery of St. Paul Outside-the-Walls] (Torino: Societa Editrice Internazionale, 1934), p. 72.

Matthiae, pp. 12, 15, 30, 36, 63-65; Plates 1-4.

Perla, pp. 43-45, 47 (describes the door of the Cathedral of Amalfi as the one commissioned toward 1062 by an *"opu-*

lento e pio" Pantaleone, at the Constantinople workshop of Simeone di Siria).

Preston, p. 65.

von Thieme and Becker, "Staurakios," vol. 31 (1937), p. 499.

Savage, p. 82.

Walicki, *"Dekoracja architektury i jej wystrój artystyczny,"* p. 228.

Zarnecki, *Romanesque Art*, pp. 120, 125.

10 Bertaux, Vol. 1, part 2, pp. 51, 407.

Bloch, Vol. 1, part 2, p. 153; Vol. 3, Figures 91-94.

Dalton, pp. 618-619.

Diehl, p. 237.

Kleinbauer, pp. 280-281.

Knapiński, p. 20.

Laging, p. 130.

Leisinger, p. 8; Plates 149-150.

Matthiae, pp. 30, 36, 91-92; Plates 67-70.

Perla, p. 47.

Preston, pp. 12-14, 45, 65.

Savage, p. 82.

11 Bertaux, Vol. 1, part 2, pp. 51 and 405.

Bloch, Vol. 1, part 1, pp. 38, 40-41, part 2, pp. 139-140, 155-156, 160-163, 167-464, 487-494; Figure D; Vol. 2, part 3, pp. 631-643; Vol. 3, Figures 110-113, 126-158.

Dalton, p. 618.

Diehl, p. 237.

Kleinbauer, pp. 280-281.

Matthiae, pp. 12-13, 20, 30, 67-71; Plates 5-15.

Perla, p. 43.

Preston, pp. 17, 66; Plate I.

Savage, p. 82; Illustration 59; mentions the bronze founder Staurachios of Byzantium as the caster of the door at the Abbey of Montecassino.

Walicki, *"Dekoracja architektury i jej wystrój artystyczny,"* p. 228.

Zarnecki, *Romanesque Art,* pp. 120 and 125.

12 Bloch, Vol. 1, part 2, pp. 151-153; Vol. 3, Figures 85-90.

Dalton, pp. 618-619.

Diehl, p. 237.

Kleinbauer, pp. 280-281.

Knapiński, pp. 19-20.

Leisinger, p. 6; Plates 124-129.

Matthiae, pp. 20, 30, 83-88; Plates 49-66.

Perla, pp. 31-33, 35-38, 43-53, 57-175 (including illustrations).

Preston, p. 66.

Savage, p. 82.

Zarnecki, *Romanesque Art,* pp. 120 and 125.

13 Bertaux, Vol. 1, part 2, pp. 51 and 407.

Bloch, Vol. 1, part 2, p. 154; Vol. 3, Figures 96-105.

Dalton, p. 619.

Diehl, p. 237.

Kleinbauer, pp. 279-291.

Knapiński, p. 20.

Laging, p. 130.

Matthiae, pp. 30, 93-95; Plates 71-80.

Perla, p. 47.

Preston, p. 67.

Walicki, *"Dekoracja architektury i jej wystrój artystyczny,"* p. 228.

Zarnecki, *Romanesque Art,* pp. 120, 125, 157.

14 & 15 Bertaux, Vol. 1, part 2, pp. 51 and 409.

Bloch, Vol. 1, part 2, pp. 164-166, 489-490; Vol. 3, Figures 114-118.

Camillo Boito, *The Basilica of St. Mark* (Venice: Ferdinand Ongania Editore, 1888), pp. 396 and 401.

Dalton, pp. 619-620.

✠

Otto Demus, *The Church of San Marco in Venice* (Washington, D.C.: The Dumbarton Oaks Research Library and Collection, Trustees for Harvard University, 1960), pp. 53 and 75.

Kleinbauer, pp. 280-281.

Laging, p. 130.

Matthiae, pp. 14-15, 20, 30, 49-51, 97-101, 103, 107; Plates 81-135.

Preston, p. 67.

Walicki, *"Dekoracja architektury i jej wystrój artystyczny,"* p. 228.

14 & 15 - same as above.

16 Bertaux, Vol. 1, part 2, pp. 51, 405-406, 408.

Bloch, Vol. 1, part 2, 141-143, 145-151; Figure C; Vol. 3, Figures 64-84.

Dalton, pp. 618-619.

Diehl, p. 237.

Kleinbauer, pp. 280-281.

Kalinowski, *"O nowo odkrytych inskrypcjach...,"* p. 398.

Laging, p. 130.

de Fleury, p. 151.

Matthiae, pp. 20, 30, 73-82; Plates 16-48.

Perla, pp. 44-47.

Preston, pp. 28, 38, 66-67; Plate II.

Walicki, *"Dekoracja architektury i jej wystrój artystyczny,"* p. 228.

Zarnecki, *Romanesque Art*, pp. 120 and 125.

Schuster, p. 72; Plate IX.

17 Bertaux. Vol. 1, part 2, pp. 51, 423-428; Figure 177.

Bloch, Vol. 1, part 2, pp. 613-626; Figure J; Vol. 3, Figures 246-275.

Diehl, p. 237.

Knapiński, pp. 25-26.

Leisinger, p. 6; Plates 108-123.

Meomartini, p. 86; Illustrations 46-47.

Preston, p. 65.

Everard M. Upjohn, Paul S. Wingert, and Jane Gaston Mahler, *History of World Art* (New York: Oxford University Press, 1949), p. 127.

Walicki, *"Dekoracja architektury i jej wystrój artystyczny,"* p. 228.

18 Giulio Carlo Argan, *L'architettura protocristiana, preromanica e romanica* [Early Christian Architecture, Pre-Romanesque and Romanesque] (Bari: Dedalo Libri, 1978), p. 59.

Bertaux, Vol. 1, part 1, pp. 345-346; part 2, pp. 51, 409-414.

von Boeckler, *Die Bronzetür von San Zeno*, p. 5.

Dalton, p. 620.

Diehl, p. 237.

Kalinowski, *"O nowo odkrytych inskrypcjach...,"* p. 398.

Kleinbauer, pp. 280-281.

Knapiński, pp. 21-22.

Leisinger, p. 8; Plates 151-152.

Matthiae, pp. 47-48, 109; Plates 136-139.

Preston, p. 65.

Walicki, *"Dekoracja architektury i jej wystrój artystyczny,"* p. 228.

Zarnecki, *Romanesque Art*, p. 125.

19 Bertaux, Vol. 1, part 2, p. 428.

von Boeckler, *Die Bronzetür von San Zeno*, p. 5.

de Bussierre, Vol. 1, pp. 137-139, 144-145.

de Fleury, pp. 150-151, 376-377.

Kleinbauer, p. 280.

Matthiae, pp. 19-20, 55.

Preston, p. 66.

Romani Ciampini, Vol. 1, pp. 239-240, 280; Plate LXXIII.

von Thieme and Becker, Vol. 33, pp. 523-524.

20 & 21 Bertaux, Vol. 1, part 2, pp. 51, 418-421, 428.

✠

von Boeckler, *Die Bronzetüren des Bonanus von Pisa und des Barisanus von Trani*, pp. 18-44, 53-70; Plates 36-96, 147-170.

Diehl, pp. 237-238.

de Fleury, p. 151.

Kalinowski, *"O nowo odkrytych inskrypcjach...,"* p. 398.

Knapiński, pp. 24-25; illustrations 22-24.

Leisinger, p. 9; Plates 153-160.

Morelowski, *"Drzwi gnieźnieńskie, ich związki ze sztuką obcą a problem rodzimości,"* p. 44.

Preston, p. 65.

von Thieme and Becker, Vol. 4 (1910), pp. 270-271; Vol. 2 (1908), pp. 500-501.

Walicki, *"Dekoracja architektury i jej wystrój artystyczny,"* p. 228.

Zarnecki, *Romanesque Art*, pp. 108, 125.

Zarnecki, *Art of the Medieval World*, p. 278.

20 same as above

21 same as above

22 von Boeckler, *Die Bronzetüren des Bonanus von Pisa und des Barisanus von Trani*, pp. 9-18; Plates 1-35.

Diehl, p. 237.

de Fleury, p. 151.

Kleinbauer, p. 280.

Knapiński, p. 25.

Künstler, pp. 134, 172; Plate 107.

Lavin, p. 71. Says the date is 1186.

Leisinger, pp. 5-6; Plates 88-107.

Preston, p. 66.

von Thieme and Becker, Vol. 4 (1910), pp. 270-271.

Walicki, *"Dekoracja architektury i jej wystrój artystyczny,"* p. 228.

Zarnecki, *Romanesque Art*, pp. 108, 125; Plate 138.

Zarnecki, *Art of the Medieval World*, p. 278.

23 von Boeckler, *Die Bronzetüren des Bonanus von Pisa und des Barisanus von Trani*, pp. 47-50; Plates 97-130.

Bertaux, Vol. 1, part 2, Plate XVIII; pp. 51, 420.

Diehl, pp. 237-238.

Goldschmidt, *Die Deutschen Bronzetüren des Frühen Mittelalters*, Plate Abb.5.

Knapiński, pp. 23-24.

Leisinger, pp. 6-7; Plates 130-136.

Morelowski, "*Drzwi gnieźnieńskie, ich związki ze sztuką obcą a problem rodzimości*," p. 44.

Preston, p. 66.

von Thieme and Becker, vol. 2 (1908), pp. 500-501.

Walicki, "*Dekoracja architektury i jej wystrój artystyczny*," p. 228.

Zarnecki, *Romanesque Art*, p. 125.

24 von Boeckler, *Die Bronzetüren des Bonanus von Pisa und des Barisanus von Trani*, pp. 51-53; Plates 131-146.

Bertaux, Vol. 1, part 1, Plate I, Figure 153; p. 364; part 2, pp. 51, 419-421, 428; Figure 176.

Diehl, pp. 237-238.

Kalinowski, "*O nowo odkrytych inskrypcjach...*," pp. 398-399.

Knapiński, p. 23.

Leisinger, pp. 7-8; Plates 143-146.

Morelowski, "*Drzwi gnieźnieńskie, ich związki ze sztuką obcą a problem rodzimości*," p. 44.

Preston, pp. 67-68 (dates the door to 1160).

von Thieme and Becker, Vol. 2 (1908), pp. 500-501.

Walicki, "*Dekoracja architektury i jej wystrój artystyczny*," p. 228.

Zarnecki, *Romanesque Art*, p. 125.

25 & 26 Bertaux, Vol. 1, part 2, pp. 51, 414-416.

Bloch, Vol. 1, part 2, pp. 553, 557-566; Figures E and F; Vol. 3, Figures 167-209.

von Boeckler, *Die Bronzetür von San Zeno*, Plate 7a.

Dalton, p. 620.

Diehl, p. 237.

Kalinowski, *"O nowo odkrytych inskrypcjach...,"* p. 399.

Knapiński, pp. 22-23; Plate 20.

Laging, p. 130.

Leisinger, p. 7; Plates 137-142.

Matthiae, p. 48.

Preston, p. 67 (credits the execution of the main door to "Oderisius Berardus").

von Thieme and Becker, Vol. 25 (1931), p. 561.

Walicki, *"Dekoracja architektury i jej wystrój artystyczny,"* p. 228.

Zarnecki, *Romanesque Art*, p. 125 (proposes that only the 1127-dated door was created by Oderisius of Benevento).

25 same as above

26 same as above

27 Dobrowolski, p. 105.

Bertaux, Vol. 1, part 2, p. 51 (compares it to the Trani door), p. 422.

Focillon, pp. 46-47; Plate 42.

Goldschmidt, *Die Deutschen Bronzetüren des Frühen Mittelalters*, pp. 26-38, 41-42; Plates LXIII-CIII (suggests the dates of 1050-1060).

Kalinowski, *"Treści ideowe i estetyczne drzwi gnieźnieńskich,* p. 10.

Kleinbauer, p. 280.

Knapiński, p. 18; Plate 18.

Laging, pp. 129-136; Plate 137. The suggested date: 1050-1065.

Leisinger, p. 4; Plates 36-57.

Morelowski, *"Drzwi gnieźnieńskie, ich związki ze sztuką obcą a problem rodzimości,"* p. 45.

Savage, p. 86.

Walicki, "*Dekoracja architektury i jej wystrój artystyczny, p.* 228.

Zarnecki, *Art of the Medieval World*, p. 175 ("early in the eleventh century").

28 Focillon, p. 46; Plate 43.

Goldschmidt, *Die Deutschen Bronzetüren des Frühen Mittelalters*, pp. 14-25, 39-41; Plates XII-LXII.

Kalinowski, "*Treści ideowe i estetyczne drzwi gnieźnieńskich*," pp. 10-11.

Kalinowski, "*O nowo odkrytych inskrypcjach...*," pp. 403-404.

Kleinbauer, p. 280.

Knapiński, p. 17; Plate 18.

Künstler, pp. 172 and 176; Plates 143-144.

Laging, pp. 129-131.

Leisinger, p. 4; Plates 12-35.

Morelowski, "*Drzwi gnieźnieńskie, ich związki ze sztuką obcą a problem rodzimości*," pp. 43-45.

Savage, pp. 85-86; Plates 60-61.

Swarzenski, p. 22; Plates 102-104, 107.

Świechowski, pp. 68 and 72.

Walicki, "*Dekoracja architektury i jej wystrój artystyczny*," p. 228.

Zarnecki, *Romanesque Art*, pp. 107-108; Plate 136.

Zarnecki, *Art of the Medieval World*, pp. 172-173, 175; Plate 174.

29 Goldschmidt, *Die Deutschen Bronzetüren des Frühen Mittelalters*, pp. 12-13, 39; Plates IX-XI.

Kalinowski, *O nowo odkrytych inskrypcjach...*," p. 398 (the inscription executed in modern times alludes to Berengerus as the creator of the door).

Knapiński, p. 17.

Laging, pp. 129-131.

Morelowski, "*Drzwi gnieźnieńskie, ich związki ze sztuką*

✠

obcą a problem rodzimości," pp. 43-45.

Savage, p. 86.

von Thieme and Becker, "Beringer," Vol. 3 (n.d.), p. 417.

Walicki, *"Dekoracja architektury i jej wystrój artystyczny,"* p. 228.

30 Askanas, *Brązowe drzwi płockie w Nowogrodzie Wielkim*, pp. 42-43; Plates 27-28.

Bertaux, Vol. 1, part 2, pp. 428-429.

von Boeckler, *Die Bronzetür von San Zeno*, pp. 5-69; Plates III/1-III/98.

Dobrowolski, p. 105.

Focillon, p. 129; Plate 88.

Kalinowski, *"Treści ideowe i estetyczne drzwi gnieźnieńskich,"* pp. 10-11.

Dmitri Kessel, *Splendors of Christendom*, commentary by Henri Peyre (Lausanne: Edita S.A., 1964), pp. 110-117, 260; Plates 111, 113, 115-117.

Künstler, pp. 134, 136, 172; Plate 128 (suggests that this bronze door was probably given its present form about 1140; its wings were reconstructed from the remains of an eleventh-century door [with relief panels of the life of Christ] destroyed in the earthquake of 1117; the panels illustrating the Old Testament scenes were added at the time of the door's reconstruction).

Laging, pp. 129-130.

Leisinger, p. 5; Plates 58-87.

Da Lisca, pp. 203-222; Figures 102-110.

Matthiae, pp. 14-15, 97-101, 103-107; Plates 81-135.

Albert Marignan, *Études sur l'histoire de l'Art italien du XIe-XIIIe siècle* [Studies of the History of Italian Art from the Eleventh to the Thirteenth Centuries] (Strasbourg: J.H. Ed. Heitz [Heitz and Mündel]), 1911, pp. 21-41.

Preston, p. 68.

Savage, p. 82.

Świechowski, p. 69.

Walicki, *"Dekoracja architektury i jej wystrój artystyczny,"* p. 228 (suggests perhaps the end of the eleventh century).

Zarnecki, *Romanesque Art,* pp. 107-108, 125; Plates 43 and 135 (dates the earlier-executed panels to 1138, suggesting that the door was probably made in Magdeburg, "which became an important center of international reputation for the casting of bronze," and where later [1152-1154] the bronze door for the Cathedral of Płock in Poland [now situated in Novgorod at the Cathedral of *Sancta Sophia*] is said to have been executed).

ILLUSTRATIONS
AND PHOTO
ACKNOWLEDGEMENTS

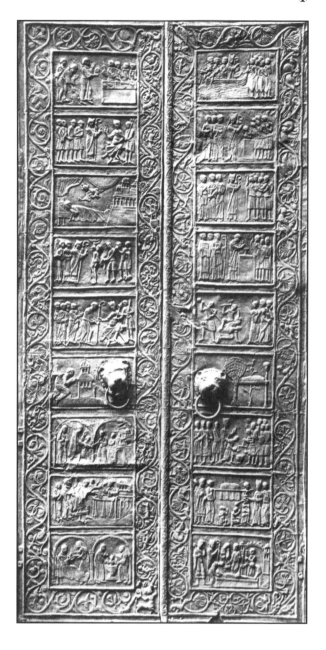

Figure 1.
(left)

Gniezno, Poland. Cathedral. View of the bronze door (1170s-1190s). (Photo: No. 60583, from Julius Kohte, *Alte Kulturstätten*, 1919; by permission Polska Akademia Nauk, Instytut Sztuki [Polish Academy of Sciences, The Art Institute], Warsaw).

Figure 2.

Gniezno, cathedral. Bronze door, fragment of the border, left wing, motif 15. (Photo: No. 61257, Mirosław Kopydłowski, from *Drzwi gnieźnieńskie* [The Gniezno Door], Michał Walicki, editor, *Dokumentacja fotograficzna* [Photographic Documentation], Vol. 3, Plate 103; by permission Polska Akademia Nauk, Instytut Sztuki, Warsaw).

Figure 3.
Gniezno, cathedral. Bronze door, fragment of the border, left wing, motif 12. (Photo: No. 61260, Mirosław Kopydłowski, from *Drzwi gnieźnieńskie*, Walicki, editor, Plate 100; by permission Polska Akademia Nauk, Instytut Sztuki, Warsaw).

Figure 4.

Gniezno, cathedral. Bronze door, fragment of
the border, right wing, motif 77. (Photo: No.
61231, Mirosław Kopydłowski, from *Drzwi
gnieźnieńskie*, Walicki, editor, Plate 148; by
permission Polska Akademia Nauk, Instytut
Sztuki, Warsaw).

Figure 5.
Gniezno, cathedral. Bronze door, fragment of
the border, right wing, motifs 65 and 66.
(Photo: No. 61302, Mirosław Kopydłowski
from *Drzwi gnieźnieńskie*, Walicki, editor,
Plate 135; by permission Polska Akademia
Nauk, Instytut Sztuki, Warsaw).

Figure 6.
Gniezno, cathedral. Bronze door, fragment of
the border, right wing, motif 70. (Photo: No.
61298, Mirosław Kopydłowski, from *Drzwi
gnieźnieńskie*, Walicki, editor, Plate 139; by
permission Polska Akademia Nauk,
Instytut Sztuki, Warsaw).

Figure 7.
(left)

Novgorod, Russia. *Sofiiskii Sobor* (The
Cathedral of *Sancta Sophia*). Bronze Door
(1152-1154) *in situ*. (Photo: Jadwiga I. Daniec,
Personal collection of Jadwiga I. Daniec).

Figure 8.

Novgorod, cathedral. Riquin (artist, bronze
casting). Bronze door, west portal, panel
detail, left wing, motif 21. (Photo: Bildarchiv
Foto Marburg / Art Resource, New York City.
SO118769, 3584, 10.4E, black-and-white print;
by permission Art Resource, New York).

Figure 9.

Novgorod, cathedral. Waismuth (artist,
bronze casting). Bronze door, west portal,
panel detail, left wing, motif 25. (Photo: Foto
Marburg/Art Resource, New York City.
SO118776, 3593, 10.4E, black-and-white print;
by permission Art Resource, New York).

Figure 10.
Novgorod, cathedral. Avraam (artist, bronze casting). Bronze door, west portal, molding detail, left wing, motif 23. (Photo: Foto Marburg / Art Resource, New York City. SO118770, 3587, 10.4E, black-and-white print; by permission Art Resource, New York).

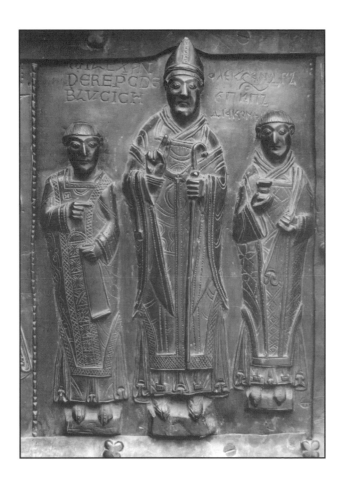

Figure 11.

Novgorod, cathedral. Alexander, the bishop
of Płock, between two deacons. Bronze door,
west portal, panel detail, left wing, motif 18.
(Photo: Foto Marburg / Art Resource, New
York City. SO118781, 3629, 10.4E, black-and-
white print; by permission Art Resource,
New York).

Figure 12.
Novgorod, cathedral. Vicmannus, the Bishop
of Magdeburg (left). Bronze door, west portal, panel detail, right wing, motif 23. (Photo:
Foto Marburg / Art Resource, New York City.
SO118775, 3614, 10.4E, black-and-white print;
by permission Art Resource, New York).

Figure 13.
Novgorod, cathedral. Bronze door, west
portal. (Photo: Foto Marburg/Art Resource,
New York City. SO118787, 3578, 10.1D, black-
and-white print; by permission Art Resource,
New York).

Figure 14.

Amalfi, Italy. Cathedral. Bronze door, west portal (1060s). (Photo: Harvey Mortimer; by permission Harvey Mortimer).

Figure 15.

Amalfi, cathedral. Cruciform. Panel detail
from bronze door. (Photo: Harvey Mortimer;
by permission Harvey Mortimer).

Figure 16.
Amalfi, cathedral. Inlaid engravings. Panel
detail from bronze door. (Photo: Harvey
Mortimer; by persmission Harvey Mortimer).

Figure 17.

Atrani, Italy. Church of San Salvatore del
Bireto. View of the bronze door, west portal
(1087). (Photo: from Hermann Leisinger,
*Romanesque Bronzes: Church Doors in Medieval
Europe*, Plate 149; by permission Europa
Verlag A.G., Zürich).

Figure 18.
Montecassino, abbey, Italy. Cloister court-
yard. (Photo: Ediz. Abbazia di Montecassino;
by permission Abbazia di Montecassino).

Figure 19.
Montecassino, abbey. View of the bronze
door (post-World War II restoration), origi-
nally 1066. (Photo: Ediz. Abbazia di
Montecassino; by permission Abbazia di
Montecassino).

Figure 20.
Monte Sant'Angelo, Italy. Sanctuary of S.
Michele sul Gargano. View of the main
bronze door (1076). (Photo: Harvey
Mortimer; by permission Harvey Mortimer).

Figure 21.
Monte Sant'Angelo, Sanctuary of S. Michele
sul Gargano. Abraham abasing himself
before the angels. Inlaid engravings. Panel
detail from main bronze door. (Photo:
Harvey Mortimer; by permission Harvey
Mortimer).

Figure 22.
Monte Sant'Angelo, Sanctuary of S. Michele
sul Gargano. Angel wrestling with Jacob.
Inlaid engravings. Panel detail from main
bronze door. (Photo: Harvey Mortimer; by
permission Harvey Mortimer).

Figure 23.
Monte Sant'Angelo. Sanctuary of S. Michele
sul Gargano. Engraved text. Panel detail
from bronze door. (Photo: Harvey Mortimer;
by permission Harvey Mortimer).

Figure 24.
Salerno, Italy. Cathedral. View of the main
bronze door (1087-1099). (Photo: Alinari/Art
Resource, New York City. SO110371,
AN26627, black-and-white print; by permis-
sion Alinari/Art Resource, New York).

Figure 25.

San Marco, Venice, Italy. Basilica. View of the main (Madonna) bronze door (1112-1138?) in the vestibule. (Photo: Alinari / Art Resource, New York City. SO110383, AL20705, black-and-white print; by permission Alinari / Art Resource, New York).

Figure 26.

San Marco, Venice. Basilica. Detail from the
side (San Clemente) bronze door at the right in
the vestibule (circa 1100). (Photo: Alinari/Art
Resource, New York City. SO110377, AL20706,
black-and-white print; by permission
Alinari/Art Resource, New York).

Figure 27.
St. Paul Outside-the-Walls, Rome, Italy.
Basilica. View of the bronze door (1070), for-
mer main entrance door. (Photo: Harvey
Mortimer; by permission Harvey Mortimer).

Figure 28.
St. Paul Outside-the-Walls, Rome. Basilica.
Panel details from bronze door. (Photo:
Harvey Mortimer; by permission
Harvey Mortimer).

Figure 29.

Benevento, Italy. Cathedral. View of the former main bronze door (1150-1200). (Photo: from Almerico Meomartini, *Benevento*, Plate 46; by permission Nuovo Istituto Italiano D'Arti Grafiche, Bergamo, Italy).

Figure 30.
Benevento, cathedral. Panel details from
bronze door, formerly main portal. (Photo:
from Meomartini, *Benevento*, Plate 47; by permission Nuovo Istituto Italiano D'Arti
Grafiche, Bergamo, Italy).

Figure 31.
(left)
Canosa di Puglia, Italy. Chapel-Mausoleum
of Bohemund I. View of the bronze door
(shortly after 1111). (Photo: Harvey
Mortimer; by permission Harvey Mortimer).

Figure 32.
Canosa di Puglia, Italy. Chapel-Mausoleum
of Bohemund I. Leonine mask. Detail from
bronze door. (Photo: Harvey Mortimer; by
permission Harvey Mortimer).

Figure 33.

St. John Lateran's Baptistery, Rome, Italy. The Pope Celestine III (?), drawing after original. Detail from bronze door (1195) to St. John's the Evangelist chapel. (Photo: from Joannis Ciampini Romani, *Vetera Monimenta* [Ancient Monuments] [Rome, 1690], p. 239, Plate LXXIII).

Figure 34.
(right)

Monreale, Sicily, Italy. Cathedral. View of the main entrance bronze door (1186). (Photo: Foto Marburg / Art Resource, New York City, SO118771, 142124, 10.1C, black-and-white print; by permission Art Resource, New York).

Figure 35.
Monreale, cathedral. View of the side bronze
door (1190). (Photo: Foto Marburg / Art
Resource, New York City. SO118772, 79493,
10.1C, black-and-white print; by permission
Art Resource, New York).

Figure 36.

Pisa, Italy. Cathedral. View of the main bronze
door (Porta di San Ranieri), 1180-1186. (Photo:
Foto Marburg / Art Resource, New York City.
SO118777, 2622, 10.1F, black-and-white print;
by permission Art Resource, New York).

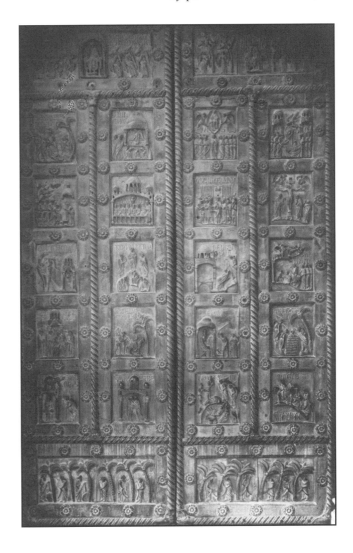

Figure 37.
Ravello, Italy. Cathedral. View of the main
bronze door (1179). (Photo: Foto Marburg / Art
Resource, New York City. SO118804, 1901,
10.1C, black-and-white print; by permission
Art Resource, New York).

Figure 38.
Trani, Italy. Cathedral. Façade. (Photo:
Harvey Mortimer; by permission
Harvey Mortimer).

Figure 39.

Trani, cathedral. View of the main bronze
door (1175). (Photo: Harvey Mortimer; by
permission Harvey Mortimer).

Figure 40.
Trani, cathedral. St. George battling dragon.
Panel detail from bronze door. (Photo:
Harvey Mortimer; by permission
Harvey Mortimer).

Figure 41.
Troia, Italy. Cathedral. Façade.
(Photo: Harvey Mortimer;
by permission Harvey Mortimer).

Figure 42.
Troia, cathedral. The main entrance bronze
door (1119). (Photo: Harvey Mortimer;
by permission Harvey Mortimer).

Figure 43.
Troia, cathedral. Door pull. Panel detail, main
bronze door, left wing. (Photo: Harvey
Mortimer; by permission Harvey Mortimer).

Figure 44.
Troia, cathedral. The side bronze door (1127),
panel details. (Photo: Harvey Mortimer;
by permission Harvey Mortimer).

Figure 45.

Augsburg, Germany. Cathedral. Bronze door
(1050-1065?), south wall. (Photo: Foto
Marburg / Art Resource, New York City.
SO118815, 5515, 10.1B, black-and-white print;
by permission Art Resource, New York).

Figure 46.

Hildesheim, Germany. Cathedral. Bronze door (1015), west wall. (Photo: Foto Marburg / Art Resource, New York City. SO118816, 10733, 10.1B, black-and-white print; by permission Art Resource, New York).

Figure 47.
Hildesheim, cathedral. Expulsion of Adam
and Eve from Paradise. Bronze door, left
wing, panel detail. (Photo: No. 109/3 [19],
Courtauld Institute of Art, University of
London; by permission The Conway Library,
Courtauld Institute of Art).

Figure 48.
Mainz, Germany. Cathedral. View of bronze
door (988-1009). (Photo: Foto Marburg / Art
Resource, New York City. SO118810, 139948,
10.1B, black-and-white print;
by permission Art Resource, New York).

Figure 49.
San Zeno Maggiore, Verona, Italy. Basilica.
Bronze door (the late ninth to the late twelfth
centuries). (Photo: Foto Marburg / Art
Resource, New York City. SO118773, 777165,
10.1C, black-and-white print; by permission
Art Resource, New York).

Figure 50.
San Zeno Maggiore, Verona. Basilica.
Expulsion of Adam and Eve from Paradise.
Panel detail, bronze door, left wing. (Photo:
No. 227/22 [36]. Courtauld Institute of Art,
University of London; by permission The
Conway Library, Courtauld Institute of Art).

——— ✠ ———
ABOUT THE AUTHOR

J adwiga Irena Daniec was born in Poland in 1916. The
daughter of a scientist and educator, she grew up in
Poland, receiving her Master of Laws degree from the
University of Warsaw. She began her legal training in
Warsaw's law courts in preparation for a judgeship, but the
German-Soviet invasion of Poland in 1939 and the outbreak
of World War II abruptly altered the direction of Mrs.
Daniec's life. Her homeland defeated, her home in Warsaw
bombarded, she and her husband Juliusz left Poland and
she has lived abroad ever since.

After making their way to America, Mrs. Daniec com-
menced her graduate study at Columbia University. Upon
earning a Master of Arts degree in art history, she contributed a number of articles and art book reviews to *The
Polish Review*, a scholarly quarterly. She has also read papers
on her field of expertise at The Polish Institute of Arts and
Sciences of America, Inc., located in New York City.

Mrs. Daniec was a longtime employee of Time Inc., and is a
naturalized U.S. citizen. *The Message of Faith and Symbol in
European Medieval Bronze Church Doors* was written in the
wake of the loss of Juliusz, Mrs. Daniec's husband of fifty-
six years. Presently, the author resides in Forest Hills, New
York.

Index of Names

A

Aaron, 125

Abbas Symon, 90
  See also Symon, the abbot

Abel, 122, 125

Abgarowicz, Kazimierz, 56

Abraham (Avraam), Table II,
  Table VIII, 71
  See also Avraam (Abraham)

Abraham (the patriarch), 125

Abraham, Władysław, 91

Adalbert, the Archbishop of
  Magdeburg, 24

Adalbert, Table III, 24, 25, 26, 39
  See also St. Adalbert
  Święty Wojciech
  Wojciech

Adam, Table VIII, 122, 124, 125

Adriatic, the, 2, 107

Agnes, the wife of Władysław II,
  the Prince of Silesia and
  Cracow, King of Poland, 95

Agricola, Georgius, 127

Alexander, *Epc De Blucich*, 72, 73,
  74, 75, 92
  See also Alexander of Malonne

Alexander of Malonne,
  the Bishop of Płock, Table II
  Table VIII, 72, 92

Alexander of Neva, the Prince
  of Novgorod, 87

Alexandra, the wife of Ziemowit IV,

Prince of Płock, 70
  See also Ziemowit IV

Alfieri, Bianca Maria, 13

Amalfi,
  the Cathedral of, Table II, 92,
  101, 104, 106, 107, 128
  the family of, 105, 106
  the town of, Table I, Table II, 2,
  105, 112

American, 8, 32, 36

Angel of the Lord, the, 107

Anglo-Saxon, 56

Anjou,
  See also Jadwiga, the wife of
  Władysław Jagiełło and
  Queen of Poland

Annunciation, the, Table VIII, 78, 110,
  116, 122, 124

Antioch, 112

Apostles, the, Table VIII, 78, 106, 109,
  110, 115, 117, 118, 119

Apulia, 100, 126

Apulian, 117, 119

Aquinas, St. Thomas, 60
  See also St. Thomas Aquinas

Argan, Giulio Carlo, 132

Aristotle, 60

Ascension, the, Table VIII, 78, 116

Aschaneus, Martinus, 86

Askanas, Kazimierz, 13, 20, 74,
  83-97, 137

✠

Z